DOMOVIK 2

Prologue

You and I, our grandfathers and sons,

avoiding mistakes, sins and guilt,

to live according to the Law of God, calling upon the people

We will move forward together for a long time.

You are such a role model among people!

My best friend, my father!

The history of the world is good, beautiful, and looks noble when people write a chronicle of events in time together: brightly, colorfully, with broad strokes, avoiding clumsy movements, giving much space in the narrative to the light of reason rather than to the dark tones of ignorance, while skillfully smoothing out sharp edges with the delicacy of culture, creating with a selfless soul a rosy, good impression that all the peoples of the world are nothing less than brothers to one another.

But at the same time, it's reasonable to clarify that among every ethnic group, there have been, are, and will undoubtedly be all manner of misguided parasites, barbarians, and fools who complicate the life of humanity with their corrupt essence. But, for the understanding of orthodoxy, the testing of Faith and convictions—perhaps they were not created in vain as creations and are also necessary?!

Walking in step in a beautiful rose garden with smiles in a pastoral utopia, hand in hand or in an embrace like lovers on a date, singing the praises of our best representatives for their honest, valiant work and success in creative endeavors is always better than marching like soldiers on a parade ground with weapons at the ready, carrying out the orders of stupid, madmen leaders or bloodthirsty leaders looking for a pretext to start a war.

And then the chronicle of human destinies becomes wretched and ugly, tinged with a sadly bloody tragedy, when it is made up on the fly for the purpose of promoting lies and disinformation by an odious graphomaniac in exotic glasses, a narcissist by nature, who loves to pick his nose and invent fairy tales.

The UN Security Council demanded yesterday that urgent reform be carried out, and that the international organization itself undergo constructive reorganization, with amendments to the charter.

All the mystical events described in the various plots of this brutally Nordic story with terrifying fragments, seemingly real, which will be discussed below, were obtained in various ways from third parties at random in various situations, after which they were simply interpreted by me in a sum total into a fictional story in order to simplify the complexity of the ornamental composition for meaningful perception and ordered for ease of information retrieval.

As an ordinary person, I had no way to verify the reliability of the information or establish its authenticity. Any possible coincidences with real people, including last names, first names, and positions described in this story, were also obtained from third parties. Please note that the author assumes no responsibility for these seemingly plausible or possibly fictitious stories.

But given that such inhumane facts are sometimes openly discussed not only in the media, but also in the parliaments of great countries, and also figure in investigations by international law enforcement agencies, including those combating the illegal removal, trafficking, and transplantation of human organs, I consider the revelation of this story to the world, albeit controversial, to be justified.

If any of my readers have had a similar sad experience in their lives, or have suffered from other violent acts that threatened their personal safety, I ask everyone to forgive me for unintentionally causing pain and unnecessary worries, and for involuntarily invading their personal spiritual space.

Sincerely yours, N.M.

Table of Contents

Prologue ii
Introduction 1
CHAPTER 1 8
CHAPTER 2 51
CHAPTER 3 74
CHAPTER 4 77
CHAPTER 5 84
CHAPTER 6 87
CHAPTER 7 90
CHAPTER 8 93
CHAPTER 9 97
CHAPTER 10 101
CHAPTER 11 106
CHAPTER 12 109
CHAPTER 13 122
CHAPTER 14 124
CHAPTER 15 136
CHAPTER 16 145
CHAPTER 17 152
CHAPTER 18 161
CHAPTER 19 173
CHAPTER 20 181

Introduction

Glory be to Allah, Lord of the worlds! Greetings and peace be upon the Lord of the Messengers, our Prophet Muhammad! May Allah bless him and greet him with everlasting blessings and greetings, lasting until the Day of Judgment!

Truly, the tales of the first generations of people became an edification for their descendants living today, the creators of their own history, so that a person could hear and see what events happened similarly to others , so that he could think and learn, so that, delving into the legends of bygone peoples and what happened to them, he would refrain from sin... Praise be to those who made the tales of ancient and modern heroes an educational lesson for subsequent peoples!

I seek refuge in Allah from the stoned devil. In the name of Allah, the Most Gracious, the Most Merciful.

No one has the right to accuse me of racism, religious-nationalist beliefs, a preference for asserting the harmonious uniqueness of Islamic culture and religion, the superiority of Turks over other ethnic groups, or, especially, hatred towards the supposedly chosen people of God.

All people descended from the prophet forefather Adam and the foremother Eva, therefore all people on earth are related to each other, and this is my life-affirming code, to which I have been faithful throughout my conscious life.

Moreover, I sincerely believe and believe that 99.9% of people in the world are like me. But with all this, let's not forget the terrible tragedy described in the divine Quran, with the horrific crime of Qabil killing his brother Habil . This story offers a more complete picture of events than the version presented in the Torah , where, how, and why Cain killed his brother Abel. And this is thought-provoking. But still, there are some wicked fools who dare to claim that the Quran is copied from the Bible... Nothing in common, except the names of the prophets. The most interesting thing here is that these liars and slanderers have never read the divine Quran themselves and have no understanding not only of the texts and meanings of the Holy Scriptures, but also of God.

Problems in the nature of human relationships have always existed, and will always exist. Without them, life is boring, and the value of the priceless Gift—taste and the desire to create—is lost! The natural infusion of a sense of beauty by Allah Almighty into His finest creation, Adam, inspired in him a creative desire to improve himself and the world around him. Man began to understand the great beauty of harmonious creativity as soon as the Almighty God, Holy and Great as He is, breathed into him of His Spirit.

But it is certain that subsequently, people, as the descendants of the forefather in the generations of their negligent representatives, are charged with this creative energy in varying quantities and quality; some have more strength and abilities, others less, therefore, each person initially should and is obliged to understand this rationally before attempting to improve the nature of others...

It's also worth remembering that the jinn Iblis, who fell from heaven, begged for a reprieve until the Day of Judgment, then promised to constantly harass people's willpower, testing and testing the Faith of Adam and his descendants in God's Law of voluntary worship with gratitude to the Creator of the heavens and the earth, the Creator of space and time. This accursed, blasphemous, stoned leader of the lost shaitans knows the weaknesses of the irrepressible nature of human nature and will constantly stir up doubts through his hapless minions among people and jinn, arousing in them abominations—envy, rage, deceit, self-interest, lies, deceit, slander, greed, stinginess, avarice, indifference, rudeness, laziness, gluttony, sleepiness, sloppiness.

The most disgusting of all evils is the lack of Faith, arrogance, mistrust, attraction to everything vicious: fornication with a craving for perversion, usury, gambling, the consumption of forbidden substances that cloud the mind with the intoxication of alcohol and drugs.

There are 76 major sins, the most serious of which are: associating partners with Allah, murder, witchcraft, failure to perform namaz, evading the payment of zakat, disobeying parents, usury, adultery and fornication, theft, lying, perjury, homosexuality, suicide, drinking blood, assimilating women to men and men to women, hypocrisy, narcissism , etc.

The most correct and infallible creative credo is to always strive to overcome your own imperfections. If you want to make the world a better place, start with yourself first.

Every person, as an individual, as a personality, is capable of always improving the world around them through constant self-improvement, developing their qualities, talents, and refining their tastes, manners, habits, and behavior. This dynamic spiritual awakening and internal development, within the static framework of sobriety and composure, must be and remain the fundamental foundation of morality, demonstrating the manifest, not merely imaginary, virtue of the human subject. And this imperative, a personal, internal code of honor, cannot be transformed into a social movement.

Ignorance is bipolar and has two centers of power; it can be a flaw on one side and a shortcoming on the other. There's no way to combat it, not on your own, not with medicine or psychology... Only by educating yourself from within: your heart, soul, and mind.

Life is full of paradoxes. What does it mean to be literate, educated, intellectual, erudite, a professor, a doctor of science, an engineer, or a scientist? What does it mean to be ignorant of religion, morality, and ethics? There are many frivolous politicians and journalists who, while not only illiterate but also completely ignorant of Muslim culture and religion , deliberately and for money accuse Islam of every conceivable and inconceivable atrocity, especially of terrorist tendencies.

And nothing can be done or undertaken against this immoral lawlessness at this time, because behind them stand the all-powerful and powerful army of invisible Zionists in the crowd, deputies in the Parliaments of the Great Countries, judges in robes, prosecutors and lawyers, bankers and financial tycoons, pot-bellied functionaries of cinema, television, radio, the Internet and all social networks, the means of communication of the IMF, WHO, FIFA, UEFA, IAEA, UNESCO, Greenpeace, literally all world organizations associated with science, sports, culture, health, food, including, of course, the Presidents of countries in one way or another connected in relations with the interests of Zionism and secret societies.

And there's no talk of conspiracy theories here; everything has already happened, and it has happened, but they just don't talk about it, they're silent. They're afraid. Everyone knows for a fact how they managed to negate the significance of Christianity. As we all know, silence is consent. But what if we dig deeper into the imperishable layers of pliable history and look impartially, without distorting the facts or the propaganda prompts of crooked, tongue-tied, bespectacled men, at the history of the world's development over the centuries? Without citing the works of hundreds of outstanding thinkers, let's take two authorities.

Abu Imran Musa ibn Maymun ibn Abd -Allah al- Qurtubi al-Yahudi , also known as Moses ben Maimon Maimonides (1135–1204), voluntarily converted to Islam, as many commentaries on the subject have written about. Some Jews now justify this by claiming that, due to his activities and high position in the Caliphate, he converted to Islam, that is, formally. He also, supposedly for effect, admitted that Islamic philosophy and culture had a strong influence on his thinking, prompting him to take many of these values and attempt to incorporate them into the Jewish worldview. Most now claim he hated Islam altogether. However, if one looks at all of Maimonides' works, one sees him solely researching and studying the works of Islamic scholars, after which he wrote appeals to his people. After studying the works of Al-Farabi on Islamic political philosophy, he even leaned toward the idea that dualism in belief is permissible, being a Muslim while remaining a Jew at heart, and even began translating his works into Hebrew.

He became fascinated with the study of Aristotle's worldview theories as a Muslim scholar . He wrote letters calling on the Jews of Morocco and Egypt to "remain strong under cultural pressure and embrace Islam." A message on apostasy.

Maimonides considered Avicenna a teacher, using his ideas on spiritual matters, metaphysics, and mysticism in his own works, and referencing them in his writings. His approach to the codification of Jewish law and philosophy was shaped by the ideas of Islamic scholars, including The Guide of the Perplexed. For centuries, this was acknowledged in assessments of the works of Rambam , but now fanatics deny it. But compare the scholar's works impartially.

He drew heavily on the values of his jurisprudence in his study of Mishnaic Law, and also followed a methodological approach in stylizing Ibn Hazm's ideas in Al- Muhalla . Abu Muhammad Ali ibn Ahmad al- Andalusi , 994–1064, Cordoba. This is undeniable.

The Muslims in the 13th century , who were numerous and could be found throughout medieval Europe. He himself had several wandering travelers as teachers: alchemists, astrologers, philosophers, and some Sufi dervishes.

According to his many notes in his writings, followers of the Islamic worldview stood out from all other religious adherents. They were like knights, distinguished by their valor, fearlessness, and military nobility, especially their respect for defeated enemy armies. They were like merchants, distinguished by their honesty and meticulousness. They were like customers, distinguished by their courtesy and generosity. They were like neighbors, distinguished by their politeness and hospitality. They were like people, distinguished by their cleanliness, attractive appearance, knowledge, and wealth.

At a more advanced age, after studying the works of Avicenna, Ibn Rushd, and after the comments of various Islamic scholars, primarily Al-Farabi, in relation to the legacy of Aristotle's worldview, Albert the Great began to call Islam the Religion of Scholars.

Here it makes sense to add what E. Renan said : Albert the Great owes everything to Avicenna (Abu Ali ibn Sina), and Saint Thomas Aquinas, as a philosopher, owes much to Averroes (Ibn Rushd).

Until the end of the 15th century, European scholars relied on and based their knowledge solely on the concepts of Islamic knowledge; for another two centuries, they continued to cite Arab scholars.

Many in their works allowed themselves to directly copy: - Leonard of Pisa (Fibonacci), rewrote from Arabic the Book of Calculations, written for children more than three hundred years ago by Al-Khwarizmi,

- Roger Bacon (Doctor Chudabilis) appropriated the works of Ibn al- Haytham (Alhazen), including those on the physics of optics, and rewrote the formula for gunpowder,

- Arnaud de Villeneuve (Arnaldus de Villa Nova), rewrote the works of Avicenna, Abu-l- Salt ,

- Raymond Lully, a simple translator from Arabic, was recognized as one of the influential original thinkers of the European Middle Ages,

Alfonso X of Castile, nicknamed the Learned Astronomer, the King of Castile and León, desired recognition as a learned scholar and appropriated the so-called Astronomical Tables to his name. In reality, this was a tiny fraction of the extensive 70 works on astronomy by Abu Rayhan al-Biruni, written several centuries earlier in the 10th century by the creator of the globe in Khorezm.

For the benefit of Europeans, it's probably necessary to clarify that, when referring to Islamic scholars, it's customary to refer to them as Arab scholars. Meanwhile, most of them are from Central Asia—Turks and Persians. But all these luminaries of science listed above are just the tip of the iceberg.

Let us recall M. Libri, who wrote frankly: "Exclude the Arabs from the history of the revival of literacy, and Europe will be late for many centuries."

CHAPTER 1

Truth belongs to God. People have their own truth, each person's own, depending on their intelligence and imagination. Truth in court, in referendums during elections, and in other collective votes so pompously called democratic, is already the truth according to the majority. Simply put, the verdict "general truth" isn't the truth, but it still transforms all other minority truths into a degree of doubt, a half-truth.

The magnitude of a person is measured by the way their life is filled with meaning that justifies their existence in the world. There are no superfluous people in this world. Every time has its space, every space has its time, and everything is absolutely subordinated to the will of God.

The evil Iblis, along with his shaitans, constantly interferes with these rules among people and jinn in order to sow evil and blasphemy through people's failure to comply with the Laws of God, in order to lead them astray from the straight path and plunge them into the sin of despair.

At all times, the prophets showed the direct path of worship to the Most High God and taught how to correctly fulfill the Law of God.

In other difficult times, when the fate of humanity was being decided, hanging by a thread: due to the spread of lies, abomination and evil in the affairs of people, vile dark ideas in their minds, the Merciful and Compassionate Allah prepared the Great Prophets and Messengers for an epochal mission to the peoples with the teachings in the books of revelation, the Holy Scripture: Torat (Torah), Zabur (Psalms), Injil (Gospel).

But since the copyists of books sometimes allowed themselves to introduce personal creativity into the books during their work, the revelations given to the prophets were distorted and lost their sanctity.

Because of this, religious parishioners were unable to understand everything on their own, and so the clergy seized spiritual power. Consequently, at best, indifference and skepticism toward the clergy reign in the public mind; at worst, complete ignorance of the knowledge and understanding of God and, consequently, the texts of Holy Scripture.

The last of the 124,000 previously sent prophets, the seal of the prophets, the Messenger Muhammad (peace and blessings of Allah be upon him), was sent with the final book of the Holy Scripture, the Quran, to all humanity. After him, there will be no more prophets, and the text of the Holy Furqan Allah, the Most Glorified and Exalted, testifies that it is in the custody of Allah, the Most High. Quran Surah Al-Hijr (15:9): "Indeed, We have sent down the Reminder, and indeed, We are its guardian." That is, the text of the Quran is protected from distortion and change for all eternity.

According to Islamic tradition, man is always at a crossroads.

The path to beauty is a movement towards high spiritual awakening and development towards the countless diversity of angels.

Attraction to evil - a fall to the level of worldview and understanding of the world in the state of thousands of animal species, giving in to base desires, stupidity, hoarding, material aspirations, living by instincts and carnal needs from an excess of desires and lust.

People of the Book! Take the Tanakh, with the entire collection of the books of the Torah, Nevi'im, Ketuvim, and, of course, the Talmud, with all its works, with and without distortions, place your hands on these sacred texts and swear that you believe in the Almighty Elohim, strive daily to live according to the divine commandments, and fulfill the Law of God to the best of your ability. Without a doubt, you will curse Zionism and execute the wicked.

People of the Book! Take the Old Testament (the Tanakh and additional sacred books), the New Testament (the Gospels of Mark, Matthew, Luke, and John, as well as the historical book: Acts of the Holy Apostles, as well as the Epistles: 21 (twenty-one epistles of various apostles, as well as the prophetic book: Revelation of John the Theologian) in your hands. Each individual denomination can take the books they believe in, with all the writings, with or without distortions of the texts. Place your hands on the sacred texts and swear that you believe in the One God, strive daily to live according to the divine commandments, and fulfill the Law of God to the best of your ability.

Now consider that all these books are sacred in Islam, and Muslims believe in them with humble devotion, observing God's Law and all prescribed commandments without fail. They believe in the Torah of the Prophet Moses without distortion or editing. They believe in the Gospel of Jesus without distortion or editing.

Islam means submission to God. Muslim means devoted to God. The essence of the faith is belief in the One God (monotheism), the voluntary worship of Allah, the Most High, Holy and Great.

The Five Pillars of Islam: Iman (shahada—the oath of faith in monotheism), namaz (fasting—the flowering of virtues during the month of Ramadan), zakat (purification of property from hoarding, a manifestation of generosity), and hajj (a pilgrimage to the first temple built by the forefather Adam, on the site where he met his foremother Eve forty years after the fall from paradise. The black stone, which fell from the sky by the command of Allah Almighty, showed the forefathers the direction of the meeting place, is embedded in the wall of the temple).

Faithful believers recognize and understand all texts of Holy Scripture as consistent with the activity of a sober mind and the purity of the heart. Islam has no idols, no statues, no altars, and therefore no priests. Therefore, Muslims are skeptical of the attempts of priests, clergy, and clergymen in all religions to act as intermediaries in communication with the Almighty God, believing that every rational person should also develop spiritual knowledge.

From this there is a scale of estimated growth: for good receipt - savapa , for allowing a sin, voluntarily or involuntarily - gunah, therefore the believer strives to receive more savapa , for this is imperishable capital.

Because a religious sacrament precludes the possibility of anyone else possessing the attributes of the Supreme God?! Nowhere in any book of Holy Scripture are there any definitions of God: power, eternity, He doesn't sleep, eat, drink, or relieve Himself, no one or anything can see Him on earth, He needs no one or anything, yet everyone needs Him. He only needs to will something, He simply says, "Be," and it happens.

Therefore, Islam denies that the Almighty God has a wife, children, other relatives, rivals, competitors, or ill-wishers. All good comes from God, and all bad comes from God.

The Almighty God created angels, jinn, and recognized the first man, Adam, as his best creation.

For God, nothing is impossible or unachievable. Therefore, Muslims believe in the immaculate conception of the Virgin Mary and consider her one of the best women on earth, and her son, the

Messiah Isa (Yeshua), a Messenger and one of the Great Prophets of Islam.

No one can accuse me of anti-Semitism. Especially considering the absurd, misleading, and always deliberately provocative use of the term anti-Semitism, specifically to create conflicts of interest.

Jews have usurped and privatized the term and are now using it in the media as a reprehensible accusatory argument, which in itself is egregious, false, and wrong. This is a question of logic and morality, for it is shameful.

Firstly, the Semites include: Arabs, Assyrians, Palestinians, Lebanese, Maltese, there are small peoples of Tigre, Amhara, Tigray , and others.

But for some reason, despite all this, Jews have appropriated anti-Semitism, completely disguising the concept. They shout about it everywhere and anywhere possible. Although they could be rightfully outraged by more offensive expressions and nicknames: kikes, Judeo-Masons, bloodsuckers of Christians, murderers of Christ.

Their penchant for fornication and perversion, for lying and deceit, their mania for blasphemy, greed, usury, gambling, indecent activities, stinginess, avarice, and deceit. All these examples of deceitfulness contradict Christianity and are especially clearly noted in the Holy Scriptures: the Torah (Torah), the Psalms (Zabur), the Gospels (Injeel), and also in the Quran.

They are described in detail in the scientific treatises of the luminaries of the fathers of history: Herodotus, Thucydides, Cicero, Bede, Spinoza, and many works of other famous scientists...

Finally, Judaism has been studied and analytically examined in the literary masterpieces of the classics: Shakespeare, Balzac, Gogol, and hundreds of other famous authors.

Zionism has flourished in all its glory, penetrating all levels of society and government through controlled media, and imposing its will on them through corruption. Now, those involved in political matters are afraid to talk about it. It's taboo.

If anyone doesn't believe me, let's see what awaits the talented man and undoubtedly Hollywood star Mel Gibson after his public apology for the alleged anti-Semitic remarks he made in a conversation with a police officer.

It was all certainly a setup, drinking, drunk driving and the honest belief that the Jews were responsible for all wars... It was revenge for the Passion of Christ.

They'll show him what's going on. It's such a great opportunity for them to show off their current strength and power to the world in all its glory. They won't miss the chance, they'll ruin his life with all sorts of problems and won't let him do what he loves.

- Evidence? - One, but absolutely indisputable one. No country in the world except Israel has the right to exist. The intelligent reader will understand.

An exception to the rule. A sacred cow in human law. This means they are above all others, which is a fact of recognition – they have appointed themselves masters of the world.

This idiocy, a savage precedent in modern times, essentially permits Zionists to murder, rape, expel from their homes, and seize the property of the Philistines (the Palestinian people, descendants of the Prophet Isaac and his eldest son, Esau) of the Holy Land. Millions of Palestinians were mercilessly murdered during these bloody decades of genocide, in the most excruciating manner as a tool of intimidation, resulting in millions fleeing their homeland and becoming refugees.

Every single day, every Palestinian experiences open hostility and xenophobia on ethnic and religious grounds from a world of embezzlers who condemn them to constant torment at the hands of Jews. This is outrageous. If we look at this systemic atrocity from all sides impartially, then there remains no concept of Humanity in the world, for this total genocide essentially erases the meaning of Morality and Ethics. The Gordian Knot has been blown.

Now the Zionists have occupied not only Palestine; they have seized, through a behind-the-scenes struggle between secret society bulldogs and family clans, leverage over all branches of government in the United States. Since the ill-conceived artificial creation of Israel by Freemasons and Anglo-Saxon Protestants, this obsession has been sucking the lifeblood of hundreds of billions of dollars from naive and gullible American citizens with each new presidential term.

Instead of improving the conditions of their personal and social life in the country, the nation, through its naive stupidity, supports the Israelis who occupy Palestine and daily subject the indigenous population to total, humiliating xenophobia on ethnic and religious grounds, putting them in a state of disenfranchisement, subjecting them to systematic, planned extermination and progressively increasing violence since 1948.

Moreover, less than half of international grant financial aid is returned in the tens of billions of dollars and deposited in Zionist foundations. It then influences the electoral system, presidential, parliamentary, judicial, and state elections, even in the United States itself.

At the same time, those who have risen to power through such a springboard, upon assuming office, are aware of this and, feeling obligated, in turn influence the enrichment of Zionist representatives in business, the financial and banking sector, culture, and sports, and their number among billionaires and multimillionaires.

Here it is necessary to clarify that Judaism and Zionism are not the same thing.

Judaism is one of the three world religions of monotheism. Monotheism is a narrow approach, an ethnic religion of God's chosen people, closed to other nations, with God's Law reserved for Jews only.

Therefore, one could say that Jews are adherents of the Jewish monotheistic religious and cultural movement. Traditionally, they try to distinguish themselves from other peoples through their appearance and the essence of their faith, and at the same time, they make no attempt to hide their contempt for Christians, but rather demonstrate it through ridicule, spitting, and a disgusted attitude toward them, as if they were animals.

They have always had a neighborly, respectful attitude toward Islam, and Muslims in particular, and there is a reason for this. As People of the Book, who have professed monotheism throughout their history, they were protected by devout Muslims in Islamic states. Arabs, Assyrians, Philistines , Lebanese, Maltese, and others considered them cousins until 1948.

The ideology of Zionism, at the beginning, not yet having acquired its clear form as a "political metropolis", not yet having subordinated to its power the intended goals of the "future colonies" of the mythical satellites of its orbit, and not having received a name, nevertheless slowly began to acquire features and form in certain circles of nobles and intellectuals.

The club, composed of noble representatives of the families, initially appeared as some kind of secret knightly order, conceived by ambitious fanatics of the new wave among the youths of elite families who had become fabulously rich from the fruits of colonialism in Hindustan and the New World.

These young, new-fangled Anglo-Saxons of Protestant persuasion, possessing untold wealth and opportunities no less than the King, but forced - suppressing their arrogance, by an effort of willpower to submit to the intolerable conservative protocol - to bow down to him.

At the same time, those with insufficient understanding of monotheism took the Jewish Tanakh as the Bible, considering other Bibles distorted. The generation consisted of energetic, creative, and healthy young men, thirsting for wealth, fame, and success. Around 1820, they began to demonstrate their potential in all its glory. Potentially fierce warriors, hardened by the vanity of their veteran fathers' tales of the valiant victory they had achieved over the armies of the Great Napoleon, dreamed of demonstrating their personal heroism somewhere (so that they could tell their descendants of their legendary victories in the future) and of savoring everything possible, even the forbidden.

They didn't understand the essence of original sin—why should they be held responsible for the whimsical misdeeds of their distant ancestors, Adam and Eve? These were young people who disdained not only the rules of etiquette but also death. Yet, for their legitimate rights as nobles and their military honor, they were ready to kill anyone at any opportunity.

During military campaigns in the form of special operations to capture countries around the world, with subsequent forced colonial subordination to the metropolis, boredom reigned in the regular professional army with its strict regulations, occasionally diluted by duels that sometimes arose for trivial reasons.

All this moral depravity led the daring creative minds of the pleasure-hungry new aristocracy to create, for fun and entertainment, what is now called sport. Initially, the name was the French "di sport," meaning "fun, amusement," with a pointed twist. Applying the accumulated knowledge gained during their studies at prestigious English universities, during long stays and the deployment of armies in field camps, they devised and invented newfangled projects for the fun of it, and to create competition to determine the winners.

Over the course of several decades, many sports with clear rules were created by collective minds, which then spread throughout the world: sailing, racing on various types of boats, rugby, football, golf, cricket, tennis, boxing, billiards, darts, snooker, curling.

They seemed to have accumulated a powerful surplus of energy, which they wanted to dedicate to their homeland. To create a new, parallel alternative to the Masonic lodge, they decided to focus on conquering the Islamic world with its incalculable riches.

To begin with, they needed to establish a foothold, a territory from which to gradually conquer, with minimal bloodshed and minimal financial outlay, vast expanses inhabited by wealthy peoples with exotic cultures and cuisines. They began to carefully study and thoroughly analyze the experience of the Crusades and determined that there was no better goal than the conquest of the Holy Land and the liberation of the holy sites of Christianity by the hands and means of the fabulously wealthy: the new nobles, bankers, and moneylenders.

Behind the scenes at social club meetings, they drank copious amounts of alcohol with Them, smoked opium and hashish, and passionately discussed the project. But these militant, ambitious Anglo-Saxon eccentrics couldn't for a second imagine that the egg in the incubator wasn't a parrot's egg for training, but a Tyrannosaurus rex .

Here, we must mention the poet who captivated the delicate chords of cold-blooded Englishmen with his dark egotism, the bearer of ideas granting all-permissiveness to select members of elite society, the great poet George Gordon Byron, who was also a peer of England, a baron, and a lord. His creative legacy after his death was significant, but it had no less an impact on the total decline of morality and ethics in high society.

Unbridled vanity, an explosive mixture acquired from birth in a noble aristocratic family, and at the same time extreme poverty, left their mark on his entire subsequent life, especially on his outstanding genius talent, which was largely wasted recklessly.

The man has tried everything and anything in the literal sense, including tasting the flesh and blood of Turkish warriors in Greece, as the fanatical knights of the Crusades once did, along with King Richard the Lionheart.

Satanic temptation seethed within him; a damned genie of the devils lived within him, enticing him to indulge in the temptations of new experiences. His vulgar antics, hysterical outbursts, ostentatious, ill-considered social actions, ignorance of the Almighty God and the religion of Monotheism, and an unbearable, outrageous, and arrogant character, coupled with his sharp intellect, eloquent tongue, and noble aristocratic roots, made him extremely famous.

Fame preceded him, leaving a long trail of rapturous reviews in people's memories. In a gray, conservative environment, in such a foggy atmosphere, both literally and figuratively, bright colors have a particularly impressive effect on the human psyche.

Thus, the silhouettes of an atheistic worldview began to emerge on the scientific horizon during the era of recklessness from 1820 to 1850. Springs of freethinking bubbled and burst forth with new springs here and there, when mythical, unsubstantiated theories became fashionable and popular in public opinion, and therefore more influential than laws. Results were not long in coming.

The precursor ideas of fascism first emerged in France in the 1970s, having developed as a project in the late 19th century. The revanchism of the old aristocracy, with its desire to restore and secure the supremacy of the elite, decided to create a new feudalism within the context of capitalism. Historical accounts of the supposed superiority of the French and their colonial policies in Asia, especially Africa, are striking in their bloodthirsty scenes of terror and violence, with the merciless and excruciating murder of many millions of people. In Algeria alone, up to one million people were killed, and approximately six million African people were enslaved and transported by ship to the Caribbean, Haiti, and the French colonies.

Until now, many African countries are de jure independent and have sovereignty, but de facto they have a conditional "independence on paper".

Fascism, as an ideological construct based on aggressive nationalism and the cult of a decisive leader, became public knowledge when the movement led by Benito Mussolini came to power in Italy in 1922. Fascist ideas also found support in other countries.

Hitler's National Socialism came to power in Germany in 1933 using these same principles, adding racial theories and anti-Semitism. In politics, fascism is commonly characterized as an ideology and a specific type of political system, defined by a specific political regime, where the sum total of ideological concepts includes notions of superiority: one's own divine chosenness, greatness—nationalism.

The key features and characteristics of fascism are particularly evident and clearly visible in Zionism, and are also evident in the 1990s "Russian World" concept, a doctrine supported by the Putin regime. In terms of many theoretically characteristic and practically identifiable features, Zionism and the Russian World symbolically perfectly fit the mold of Hitler's Nazi regime, particularly in their methods of propagating lies and carefully injecting disinformation into public opinion.

Convinced atheists Karl Heinrich Marx (Herschel Levi Mordechai) and Friedrich Engels co-authored the Communist Manifesto in 1948. This blasphemous utopian idea confused the minds of the poor creative intelligentsia and the proletariat—the illiterate workers and peasants—for decades to come. It was a program for exploiting the most naive. Commissioned by Anglo-Saxon Freemasons and industrialists, the son of a rabbi, Karl Marx, wrote Das Kapital: A Critique of Political Economy. Volume 1 was published during his lifetime in 1867.

The second volume was published posthumously in 1885, the third in 1894.

The fourth volume of The Theory of Surplus Value was edited and published by Karl Kautsky in 1905.

Charles Darwin, in his theory of evolution, shows the world the path of natural selection with four progressive and weighty provisions.

In nature, more individuals are always born between species than can survive, so only the strongest can survive.

There is always a struggle for existence in life.

Within each species, individuals exhibit variability.

Offspring always inherit the traits of their parents.

Here I've presented the formula in a visually appealing form, and it can be interpreted in various ways. Therefore, you need to add lemon to the cocktail...

In his 1871 work, The Descent of Man and Selection in Relation to Relation, Darwin theorized that women, on average, are mentally inferior to men due to natural selection, which left male abilities (intelligence, ingenuity) more developed, while female qualities (emotionality) were important for the survival of the species through caring for offspring.

These views led irreversibly to the idea that all species of living beings descended from a single common ancestor on Earth, which led to the idea that humans and apes descended from a single primate stock.

Renowned scientists have united in the upper echelons of the elite against the dogma of the Bible and the Church about God creating the forefather Adam.

Atheists were thus given freedom of action.

Then, in a climate of extreme tension and irritability between the two irreconcilable adversaries (passions were stoked unbeknownst to the public by conspiring Judeo-Masonic psychologists and various charlatans allegedly possessing evil spirits), in order to prevent a possible spark from igniting a civil war between believers and atheists, a Round Table was established between the secular authorities and the Christian churches and a debriefing was conducted. In the interests of the public, this issue was divided into a stalemate—that is, the table was divided equally, and each could work on their half at their own discretion. The status quo was intended to transform Christianity into a sham.

At this time, colonialism was particularly rampant, and on American plantations, thousands of Black men, women, and children died daily from intolerable conditions, beatings, humiliating violence, and backbreaking labor, and they didn't live to old age. Again, to each their own.

All these revolutionary ideas and problems of the existence of societies left their mark on the progressive minds of the majority of the thinking and the percentage of the thinking population.

Public opinion has become dependent on newspapers and magazines.

The first to painstakingly prepare cadres were the Masonic lodges and bourgeois industrialists for the purpose of promoting their importance and advertising their goods and services.

Meanwhile, the inquisitive minds of the Jews had long been weaving a web of intrigue, seeking benefits in all ideas and concepts, like remora fish in a school of sharks.

They have lived since time immemorial in diasporas within other peoples, feeding on their vitality in many countries. When their numbers increased, they always united into a single community—the Ghetto, as they called their neighborhoods—where they always lived by their own canons and rules, obeying their elders and rabbis.

For example, typical neighborhoods can be observed in New York City, like the ghetto areas of Williamsburg or Borough Park. There, life is regulated by their own internal ethnic laws, and they have their own law enforcement agencies. All generally accepted secular laws and rules are irrelevant to them; they live by their own instincts.

Is psychology a humanities science? Psychology is the soul, logos is the teaching. A simple explanation. It's impossible to study the patterns of the emergence, development, and functioning of the psyche, the mental activity of an individual, much less groups of people. Absolutely impossible.

Psychology supposedly combines the humanities and natural sciences. This is a blatant collection of casuistry, a fraud, as if it were inadvertently turning on a light bulb when needed, like electricity during tests, claiming to be an axiom. Maybe, perhaps, it shouldn't be recognized as science. I don't impose my personal opinion.

In this metaphysics of meanings, it is better to focus on the concepts of the difference in the existence of time in space and space in time, like macrocosm and microcosm: there is the time of angels, genies and people.

Psychoanalysis encroaches on the concept of divine providence. This is not only because Jews and Zionists have no concept of Heaven and Hell, but also because (as rumor has circulated since time immemorial, and which is confirmed daily in the news) they always hide behind empty rhetoric their secret, insidious plans and selfish goals, most importantly, their inexplicable, savage bloodthirstiness. The shedding of blood, especially that of Christian children (as evidenced by numerous trials held in medieval European countries), is for them a miraculous elixir, a panacea for all their ills.

Apparently, this is why all the tricks of their psychics are aimed at causing more divorces, pitting the husband against the wife, the wife against the interests of the family, all so that the children suffer.

Ordinary Zionists are also vigilant in their contributions. Each is moving along their own path toward the ultimate goal of world domination, using their tools of influence as circumstances dictate in attempts to discredit parties, movement leaders, scientists, figures, authorities in various fields, heroes, and upstanding citizens: members of parliament, teachers, doctors, and clergy known for their virtue.

Sophisticated techniques against public interests, all sorts of dirty tricks in small steps, the favorite methods of parasites.

They have succeeded in doing something nasty on the sly, creating domestic conflict and discomfort throughout their history.

Based on this, we can already confidently assert that they will use the Internet only to the detriment of universal human values, creating tensions everywhere on social media, especially in religious disputes and, of course, historical topics with interethnic and interethnic problems.

They will especially escalate the situation in the world by creating ugly pictures of the perception of the Islamic worldview in public opinion throughout the world, presenting all these true values as evil, threats, dangers, madness, fanaticism.

They can do everything.

Even the fact that they alone reaped previously unimaginable dividends from the horrific 9/11 terrorist attack, were able to assign blame without trial (violating key provisions of US law), without open investigations or forensic examinations, and to unleash the people's wrath through a crusade to murder millions of civilians in Islamic countries and turn the millions who remained alive into disenfranchised refugees.

All at the behest of the insidious, bloodthirsty masters of Zionist intrigue.

They were in such a hurry that even a conventional international criminal, a general, diplomat, statesman, and, above all, an honest man, Colin Powell, who was never accused of committing crimes against humanity, under the collective pressure of the Zionists, committed a forgery and recklessly presented a vile, false, and slanderous report to the UN Security Council.

And for these millions of murders and the tragedy of tens of millions of Muslims , which continues to this day, no one has received the punishment they deserve.

And such masters of bloodshed as the sadistic Benjamin Netanyahu , after such a massive evil, will next create a planetary horror. The Zionists' plans have hit the wall of the Islamic worldview. And they are certainly preparing a major bomb to detonate. There are so many intelligence agencies in the world, equipped with specialized technical means, trained to conduct surveillance, obtain evidence, investigate crime scenes, conduct interrogations, find alibis, analyze events holistically from various angles, and seek out the beneficiaries of all acts of intimidation, disasters, and terrorist attacks. Yet, how could anyone even theoretically suspect that perhaps the masterminds and perpetrators could be found in Israel? It's no secret that everything about the 9/11 terrorist attack can be learned in full from Netanyahu, Sharon, and Powell.

My Armenian friend Artashes, returning from a pilgrimage to Jerusalem, indignantly declares: "The cries of children are sweeter to them than beautiful music."

"Who disagrees with me? Think about and comprehend my arguments, then evaluate their logic. This cannot be denied. Water wears away stone drop by drop. And these bugs manage to miraculously run dry between the raindrops. They have mastered the techniques of corruption, all manner of artful persuasion: in the media, in printed materials, on the internet, and have also introduced many destructive elements of doubt into school textbooks for children of all ages, modernizing Goebbels's technique by changing the percentages of propaganda and disinformation spreading in the theme of inciting hostility between monotheistic Christianity and Islam."

Their entire Jesuitical policy consists of constantly presenting information based on the figures 90% and 10%—that is, 90% is accurate information, 10% is filth, a lie. Now compare this ratio with the concept of bed linen or the condition of a patient during a doctor's examination. Bed linen should evoke disgust, and the patient is more alive than dead, but does not inspire optimism.

Now, based on all of the above, how does Zionism differ from the Nazism of Hitler? The Führer. Most people, illiterate in understanding the concepts of God and religion, who have not mastered and experienced the texts of the Holy Scriptures—the Torah, Psalms, Gospels, and the Quran—will not be able to resist the psychological hypnosis and coding of the Zionists for long.

Moreover, the concept of psychoanalysis is a clever trick, a disgusting fraud, a special operation by the Zionists, the famous financial moguls, and the World Jewish Congress to seize power in Congress and the judicial system in the United States, Europe, and Russia. These venerable crooks still dare to teach how to live correctly, creating all sorts of teachings, schools, and courses.

Compare these champions of life, living at the expense of other religions and peoples, usurers, vigilantly watching like vultures where something has become crooked, cracked, faded, where there has been a disagreement, a quarrel, where a scientific luminary or new technology appears, wherever they interfere with their insidious interest.

Everywhere and everywhere they loom, the idea of being "chosen by God" and fanaticism looms, a dream: to kill every single Palestinian "terrorist," to conquer the Holy Land, to destroy the Al-Aqsa

Mosque, to build a temple in its place, so that from there the one-eyed Messiah can rule over the entire world.

I remember once, closer to 2000, we were reviewing the doctoral dissertation of a certain Alen Grigoryan or Vardanyan, I don't remember exactly. I spent almost a month deciphering the textual presentation of this voluminous material, while the mathematician Igor Vanshtein was solving conceptual puzzles. We were sitting in a chic Uzbek restaurant in Izmailovo, having lunch with champagne, discussing the work with the author. I found numerous spelling and grammar errors, corrected them all in pencil, and delicately explained to the candidate: what, why, and how. He raised a toast, thanked me warmly, left the table, and came over to hug and shake my hand for his help. Vanshtein, however, limited himself to mere praise. He praised the introduction, the development, and especially the thoughts in the conclusion, saying that everything was clear, understandable, and masterfully explained.

The Armenian beamed, his back straight, sitting like a monument, his eyes sparkling with happiness, his forehead covered in sweat, and a large drop hanging unattractively from his nose. But our hero was apparently a lucky man today and didn't pay any attention to anything. So , as expected, he handed me the envelope containing the agreed-upon sum, and the same to Weinstein.

We left the restaurant at dusk. My car pulled up. Igor asked me to give him a ride to Neglinka, not far from the Teatralnaya metro station.

"He says he drank one champagne out of two because he was hungover. We had a wonderful time at a banquet in a Beijing restaurant yesterday. That Armenian just paid me double for the review, and I haven't even read his work yet."

- I asked again, - What do you mean? - Don't understand?

He replies, "There was no time. I just looked here and there. The work was raw, it needed drying, too much fuss, no time between judgments. So I spurred on with all sorts of praise. A good word pleases even a cat. The Armenian has blossomed, and you see how he appreciates my modest work. You'll see. He'll defend himself and throw me some money. No, then he'll come and bow to me again." "This is the law of wisdom, Zion, when all nations come to bow to you!"

Rinat, the driver, looked at me questioningly, and I said, "Let's go... We'll waste at least an hour and a half there and back if there's no traffic. I have another business meeting in an hour, right here."

Igor had gotten emotional while drunk, suddenly opening up out of nowhere. A man nicknamed "the fatty ," he was a notorious tightwad. He constantly praised Judaism and Zionism, and talked about kosher food. At the same time, he ate pork with relish, drank all kinds of alcohol, consumed all kinds of drugs, and was a sucker for any easily accessible woman of any age and appearance. His manners were appalling; he was unkempt and untidy; sitting next to him at a meal was a challenge, for he ate defiantly, as if he'd never eaten before.

But despite all this, he had extensive connections and was a liaison in the corrupt machinery of many dubious affairs. He mastered the satanic instrument of temptation—the ability to speak pleasant words in evasive phrases.

Later, rumors circulated that he was arrested as a spy for US and Israeli intelligence, then allegedly exchanged for two arms dealers. It doesn't matter what or how. But I remember that he fiercely hated the Palestinians, because he was convinced they had never lived there and that they weren't Semites. There are many such paradoxes among Jews around the world. Many are clearly mentally ill for generations.

They achieve everything by hook or by crook. They already have influence over presidents and monarchs, and they manipulate the Nobel Committee, Academy Award winners, radio, print media, book publishing houses, the internet, and Oscar, Grammy, and other award winners. This is unconventional practice.

In the second half of the 19th century, the Anglo-Saxons, while still grieving the loss of the New World, nevertheless devised new ways to govern the states from a distance, dreaming in their deepest dreams of the possibility of commanding new powerful figures represented in all the elite societies of Europe and America: the Rothschilds, the Rockefellers, etc.

They launched the political tool of Jewish emancipation and waited for someone to emerge from the seething storm of energy with an idea that could be useful to them, the Protestants. By the mid- 19th century, the idea of Jewish assimilation had completely failed in Europe; many monarchies sought new ways to more effectively manage their subjects, bankers, various entrepreneurs, and Jewish representatives in the arts.

The interests of traditionalists of monarchical systems, the far-sighted goals of secret elite societies, found common ground with the Jewish world following the results of the Hungarian Jewish Congress of 1868–1869.

Despite the split in the Jewish community between traditionalist Orthodox and modernist neologs , it was clear that the struggle of ideas would greatly benefit the Jewish people in the long term, leading to the evolution of ideas. Soon, a third faction, the "status quo," emerged in the community's struggle over which path to take, left without a supreme authority.

in Pest , Hungary, into a wealthy family of neologists . He studied at the University of Vienna. He attempted to pursue a legal career in Vienna, but after frequent conversations with family and friends about the anti-Jewish sentiments within the Austrian Empire, he decided to move. He moved to France and, in Paris, became a journalist for the Viennese newspaper Neue Svobodnaje Presse.

Even then, in private, he passionately argued to his colleagues that Christian anti-Jewish sentiments made Jewish assimilation impossible, and that Great Britain would benefit from exploiting Jewish power to dominate the world's modern history.

This requires the creation of a Jewish state, which is also the only solution to the Jewish question. This will make it possible to enslave Asian and African countries and colonize vast territories with large pagan populations.

In 1896, Herzl wrote a pamphlet, "Appeal to the Rothschilds," with which he planned to present to the banking dynasty the idea of the need for a homeland for the Jews...

However, this idea displeased Baron Edmond de Rothschild, who saw it as a potential provocation against the Jewish diaspora in Europe. It would also hinder the clan's secret plans to seize Palestine, as promised by influential figures in the House of Lords and members of the royal family. He resisted, and the audience never took place.

Then, on the advice of his young, ambitious English aristocratic acquaintances, Theodor Herzl published a pamphlet, changing the title to "The State of the Jews." His idea of a state for the Jews, which would simultaneously solve the Jewish question, attracted international political attention, and Herzl immediately became a significant figure among the Jewish people. Enormous amounts of money, in the form of donations, sponsorships, and patronage, flowed in daily from all directions.

In 1897, Herzl convened the First Zionist Congress in Basel, Switzerland. Unopposed, he was ceremoniously elected President of the Zionist Organization. Taking advantage of this prestigious position and his enormous financial resources to gain recognition, he began searching for influential Jews in every European country with whom he planned to establish mutually beneficial ties. Having established secret contacts, he and this influential group began to develop diplomatic initiatives to shape public opinion among the elites of the great powers in support of the need for a Jewish state. Money flowed in to bribe officials.

In all the hobby clubs frequented by members of high society in the US and European capitals, where everything had long been in the hands of bankers, loan sharks, financial moguls who owned casinos, theaters, and circuses, swindlers and blackmailers, mafia bosses, and criminals, one could hear passionate conversations everywhere about how Europe needed to get rid of the Jews. And most interestingly, all these clubs were invariably sponsored by famous magnate families: the Rothschilds, the Adlers , the Epsteins, the Joffes, the Warburgs , the Schiffs, the Loebs , the Sassoons , the Gunzburgs , the Ephrussis, and the Goldsmiths. Soon, new dynasties of financial mogul sponsors of the New Israel would emerge: the Rockefellers , the Welsh Morgans, and the odious French-American Protestant Du Pont family, who for decades had been obsessed with the idea of their idol, Napoleon Bonaparte, who restored the Catholic Church, amnestied the old aristocracy, placed the education system under state control, liquidated opposition parties, and proclaimed the re-establishment of a New Israel under Huguenot Protestant rule as one of the goals of his campaign in Egypt and Palestine.

In mid-March 1799, rumors circulated throughout the Jewish diaspora that the young General Napoleon was conducting a military campaign in Syria to restore Jewish statehood and rights to Palestine. A Parisian newspaper later published an article on the subject, but the newspaper later apologized for the error; the information was untrue. In late April 1799, leaflets appeared in the small Syrian diaspora, claiming the future emperor had written an "appeal to the Jews" of Asia and Africa, calling on wealthy Jews to rebuild Jerusalem. Unknown swindlers of this wily people made a tidy profit from this forgery and disappeared. But the rumors persisted.

Napoleon's 13,000-strong army failed to conquer Palestine, and Jerusalem in particular. This victory was thwarted by the heroism of a limited Turkish force led by Ahmad al- Jazzar , the viceroy of the

Ottoman Sultan Selim III, who managed to defend the Holy Land of the Philistines and the holy sites of Beit al-Muqaddas (Jerusalem).

A tradition that has been consistently preserved throughout history is the experience of judgment about the world and life, and the development plans of God's chosen people, within the three factions of religious and social groups of world Jewry. This norm has always and everywhere remained mandatory (since the ancient division into Pharisees, Sadducees, and Levites).

In the struggle of opinions, they advance "one step back and two steps forward" their routes to the final goal (world domination over the goyim) in three different routes, pre-planned along the way.

Between supposedly ardent adversaries, reliable secret communications always exist. This way, they can change tactics when implementing plans, navigate various situations, and consistently pursue their strategic goals. In any endeavor, this brings them real advantages, for other nations fail to understand the benefits of the millennia-old experience of a persecuted people, strange in appearance and dressed in exotic attire, and accept all their scenarios at face value as elements of a democratic society.

In reality, it's a scam. All the arguments, shouting, tears, and jostling are just theater; they turn the whole world into silent spectators.

All three factions decided to use their influence to support the idea of creating a New Israel. They considered options: Crimea under Tsarist Russia, Ukraine, Siberia, and the Kokand Khanate, which had become a protectorate of the Russian Tsar. Then, in the Soviet Union, they would stage an artificial Holodomor in Ukraine and Kazakhstan to facilitate the creation of a New Israel.

In 1825, Jewish-American Mordecai Manuel Noah made a desperate attempt to establish a semblance of a Jewish colony in New York City, even coining the name "Ararat." His seriousness was so fanatical that he used his own funds to purchase land on Grand

Island for $4.40 per acre to develop the project, intending to establish a colony of refuge for all his Jewish brethren.

Since Jews are not accustomed to daily, heavy, independent physical labor in agriculture and urban conditions, they need to exploit the goyim; the idea of starting from scratch and living in isolation did not appeal to them.

Then Noah, the first of the historically known individuals of Jewish descent, conceived the ambitious project of resettling Jews in Palestine, from where, according to rumors and oral traditions, they had been expelled almost two thousand years earlier during and after the Roman conquest. In essence, he was a kind of pioneer, a precursor to Zionism.

In the mid-19th century, Jewish communities in the United States proposed establishing a Jewish colony, New Israel, with a feasible project to be implemented in Alaska. However, this sensible proposal failed to gain significant support in Congress, as an all-powerful, corrupt lobby had not yet been established in Parliament.

In 1903, British Colonial Secretary Joseph Chamberlain proposed the creation of a New Israel for the Jewish community in Madagascar. The idea was initially welcomed, but after discussion, it was rejected by the Jewish community.

In 1903, British Colonial Secretary Joseph Chamberlain proposed to the Jewish side to create a Jewish colony of New Israel on the Sinai Peninsula.

In 1903, the British Colonial Secretary proposed to Theodore Herzl and his newly formed group of Zionist militants the creation of a Jewish colony in Uganda, under which part of the East African protectorate would be placed under the control of the Jewish people. The plan allocated the Jewish state an area of 13,000 kilometers on the Mau Escarpment, which is today's Kenya.

In 1904, a three-person delegation, accompanied by an armed guard of British officers and soldiers, was sent to the plateau. The Jews were horrified by the dangerous nature of this land, home to the courageous and fearless Maasai, and infested with lions and other dangerous predators. After discussing a detailed report and recognizing that such extreme conditions, with their constant testing of cowardice, could be a hindrance to mass resettlement, the World Jewish Congress, with a thousand subtleties, politely rejected the British proposal in 1905.

In the early 1920s, the Soviet leadership, largely made up of Jews, decided to create a colony, New Israel, for Jews on the Crimean peninsula.

For example, the first Politburo composition: Stalin (Georgian), Lenin (father Ilya Nikolaevich Ulyanov Russian, mother Maria Alexandrovna Blank - her father was a baptized Jew, and her mother was a German from Latvia), Trotsky (Jew Lev Brondstein), Zinoviev (Jew Ovsey-Gershen Aronovich Radomylsky), Kamenev (Jew Lev Rosenfeld). Sverdlov Chairman of the All-Russian Central Executive Committee, one of the leaders of the October Revolution, formally the head of state of the RSFSR (Jew Yankel Movshevich) Sverdov). Let's note that these were the most important leaders of the Soviet Union; no one will argue with that.

Jewish agricultural settlements had already begun to be established successfully. In 1922, the first Jewish settlers arrived, including several families from Poland. By 1924, several Jewish agricultural settlements had appeared in Crimea.

From 1925 to 1927, the Politburo discussed Stalin's idea of establishing a Jewish autonomy in Crimea, including Sevastopol, but the members of the Politburo did not support the General Secretary's proposal. The alleged problem arose with the Jewish diasporas in Ukraine and Belarus, the mountain diasporas in the Caucasus, and the Bukharan Jews in Central Asia. Few of them were willing to leave their established homes, where everyone had easy labor (a stable daily income), and no one wanted to do menial labor in the fields.

Stalin would eventually avenge this sabotage. In 1944, members of the Jewish Anti-Fascist Committee attempted to revive the project of Jewish autonomy in Crimea. But the Politburo members were all against it. They were already secretly dreaming of rapidly building communism in the Holy Land of Palestine, and from there, throughout the West—with the wily and selfish experience, the steady hands trained to blow up and fire any weapon, and the intelligence of seasoned Jewish communists and sympathizers, to begin destroying the West.

Stalin and his associates had one plan: world revolution. But the Zionists outsmarted the leader of the world revolution and even plotted a conspiracy.

On March 28, 1928, the Presidium of the Central Executive Committee of the USSR adopted the Resolution "On the allocation of free territory for the Komzet for the settlement of Jewish workers near the Amur River in the Far East."

On August 20, 1930, the Central Executive Committee of the RSFSR unanimously adopted a resolution "On the creation of the Birobidzhan National Okrug as part of the Far Eastern Territory."

In 1938, with the formation of Khabarovsk Krai, the Jewish Autonomous Oblast automatically became part of it. To eliminate perceived threats to the Soviet state in the future development of socialism, Judaism, which contradicted the official state policy of atheism, and Zionism were banned. Therefore, Yiddish, not Hebrew, would become the national language, and literature and art would replace religion as cultural expressions.

From 1933 to 1939, some of Hitler's main patrons were Jewish magnates, who encouraged and financed the Führer's insane projects in every possible way. They primarily wanted him to help expel the Jewish people from the Reich. They themselves vigorously promoted a move to Palestine, the Promised Land. This continued until Germany invaded Poland.

The Madagascar plan for the forced resettlement of Jews was proposed to Nazi Germany by Nazi ideologists Hermann Göring, Julius Streicher and Joachim von Ribbentrop in 1938. It was reviewed in June 1940. With Adolf Hitler's approval, on August 15, 1940, Otto Adolf Eichmann, head of Department IV D 4, then IV B 4 ("Eichmann Department" or "Jewish Department") of the Reich Main Security Office published a memorandum, the details of which had been secretly agreed upon with the elite of the Jewish people.

The plan was to resettle a million Jews a year for four years. The island was to become a model cultural colony modeled on a police state, initially under the control of the SS. But the problem was that wealthy Jews could not part with their stores, shops, banks, pawnshops, doctors' offices, jewelry workshops, salons, workshops, property, and warehouses, as well as, of course, comfortable housing in the cities.

They were difficult to coerce and continually eluded the effects of new restrictions on rights.

Communications have always existed between interested parties. The Central Archives of the USSR Ministry of Defense, the USSR KGB, and other security agencies, as well as the Departmental Archives, contain classified information on military operations, intelligence, and counterintelligence.

I personally read various documents, as well as the minutes of official meetings of the Congress of Jews, the Jewish Anti-Corruption Committee, denunciations of Jewish spies who worked as advisers and assistants to famous Jewish financiers, in well-known Jewish organizations, and secret meetings and discussions with Nazi representatives in the World Congress.

There are immoral agreements regarding systematic persecution, including mass arrests of Jewish citizens for failure to comply with onerous regulations and orders. Everything was done by agreement: to expel them by any means necessary, using coercive methods of systemic pressure, in order to force a voluntary exodus of Jews from Germany, then Austria, and Hungary.

But wealthy Jews always found ways to communicate with poor German citizens through monetary means and always managed to avoid fines for violations. Based on numerous documents containing shameful texts, one might conclude that all these persecutions, which escalated into numerous obvious instances of the Nazi Reich's inhumane treatment of Jews from 1933 onward, initially arose from the shadowy initiatives of multimillionaire financiers, a conspiracy by the leadership of the World Jewish Congress, and, of course, the JAC (Jewish Anti-Fascist Committee), founded in 1942 under the Soviet Information Bureau.

So, here are the numbers. At a closed meeting of senior Soviet officials on September 2, 1944, it was stated that from 1933 to 1942, in Europe, beginning with Germany, Austria, Hungary, and especially Poland and Ukraine, hundreds of thousands of Jewish families changed their names, nationalities, and obtained new passports through various criminal means.

These reports had previously been discussed at closed meetings of the Jewish Anti-Corruption Committee three times in 1942, which led to the disgrace of Polina Semyonovna Zhemchuzhina (Peri "Pearl" Solomonovna Karpovskaya, wife of Foreign Minister V.M. Molotov) in 1949. She held high positions in the USSR despite the fact that in 1918, her brother and sister emigrated to Palestine on assignment from the Political Bureau to maintain direct contact with the World Jewish Congress. The Karpovsky family launched numerous initiatives for international support of Jewish immigrants at the expense of the Soviet Union for the establishment of Israel in Palestine, but the USSR reaped no benefit from this project.

The story of Vyacheslav Mikhailovich Molotov himself (there is information that his real identity is supposedly that of Samuil Markovich Braude, but thanks to the efforts of his senior comrade Stalin, who obtained the biographical information of a certain Scriabin, along with two brothers and three sisters, for added credibility) is very strange and colorful; it is probably not for nothing that British Prime Minister W. Churchill called him a soulless, intractable robot.

Since the resettlement in Germany had failed completely by 1942, 300,000 Jews out of approximately 550,000 had left, leaving mostly families of below-average means. Due to this failure, the "territorial solution of the Jewish question" was transformed in favor of the "final solution." To intimidate the Jewish masses, it was intended to begin with planned, selective extermination in hospitals, orphanages, homes for the elderly, the disabled, the crippled, the bedridden, dwarfs, midgets, morons, cretins, the mentally ill, and those with mental disabilities. In prison medical centers and penal colonies, criminal elements were to be eliminated: cannibals, homosexuals, murderers, rapists, maniacs, thieves, swindlers, fraudsters, parasites, and swindlers.

When this instrument failed to produce adequate results within two months, it was decided to gradually begin mass arrests, selectively detaining the poor in the Ghetto, where they lived in dire poverty. At this time, wealthy Jews had many opportunities to painlessly flee Germany with their fortunes.

Please note that there is a misinterpretation of the creation of concentration camps due to inaccurate reporting by biased Zionist media. Concentration camps were established as early as 1933, long before the persecution of the Jewish population of Germany began. The main types of Nazi camps were:

. early camps,

. concentration camps,

. Zigeunerlager (Gypsy camps),

. forced labor camps,

After 1942 the following appeared:

. prisoner of war camps,

. transit camps and collection camps for Jews,

. camps of mass extermination (death camps).

Concentration camps were specifically designed as centers for the mass incarceration and detention of individuals who had not accepted fascist ideology, resisted, or were suspected of political opposition to the Nazi regime. By 1939, seven major concentration camps had been established in Germany: Dachau, Sachsenhausen, Buchenwald, Neuengamme , Flussenbürg , Mauthausen, and Ravensbrück.

By the time all suspected oppositionists had been apprehended, the Nazis had expanded the concentration camps and built new barracks. Arrested Jews who had violated regulations and rules began to be assigned to them from distribution centers, according to strict accounting. The plan was for them to pay for their forced detention through physical labor, and after serving their sentences or for exemplary work, they would be rehabilitated and released. They were transferred to barracks under armed guard.

But it wasn't always possible to provide work for everyone; the number of prisoners grew, and the treasury began to strain due to the forced, constant subsidies for the upkeep of prisoners. Sponsorship from prominent financiers ceased in 1942 due to the German government's collapse and the situation spiraling out of control, ending the Nazi leaders' secret connections and communications with world Jewry.

All the horrors of detention in concentration camps became known in the media, and witnesses emerged of how the terminally ill, the underdeveloped, and those with mental disabilities were killed.

Conditions and nutrition for prisoners in the camps steadily worsened, and by the winter of 1943, the death toll had risen. Burial according to Jewish rites became impossible because Jews no longer came to claim the bodies. Crematoria were built in the concentration camps to incinerate the bodies.

The murder of one person is a terrible crime, and talking about the mass murder of people as a crime is generally hard on the mind and heart, but statistics are a science.

There is reason and in relation to all existing mass crimes based on alleged ethnic-religious superiority and hence hatred towards those inferior on any grounds, it is always necessary to approach them with precise figures.

In addition, Hitler's Nazis built death camps throughout the conquered territories from 1939 to 1944, especially in Poland, where they established six death camps: Chelmno , Auschwitz, Belzec , Sobibor, Treblinka and Majdanek.

Furthermore, after the attack, the Nazis established killing centers near several cities in the territories captured from the USSR, where tens of thousands of people were murdered in each. The most famous are Babi Yar in Kiev, Fort IX in Kaunas, the Rumbula and Bikernieki forests in Riga, Ponary on the outskirts of Vilnius, and Maly Trostenets in Minsk. Concentration camps were also established in the occupied territories of the USSR (Salapsis) , France (Drancy) , the Netherlands (Westerbork) , Yugoslavia (Jasenovac) , Hungary (Budapest), and Romania (Transnistria).

There's no doubt about it: if the archives of the USSR, the Vatican, Great Britain, France, Turkey, Italy, and, of course, the United States were declassified, the Holocaust death toll would undoubtedly be significantly lower. Jews love to read the works of their authorities on questions of uniqueness and God's chosenness, but even more than that, they love to speculate about things that haven't yet happened, to imagine absurd scenarios of possible horrors and conspiracies against them.

Just as they invested so much effort in print media, radio broadcasts, the film industry, and, of course, money, into promoting the topic of the Genocide and Holocaust, they are now investing the same amount of effort into denying the Genocide and Holocaust of the Palestinian people, which Israel is openly perpetrating.

Apparently, these types of blatant double standards don't bother them. They close their eyes and ears, occasionally creating all sorts of generously paid provocations using disenfranchised, servile mercenaries from among the indigenous population, only to then shout to the world that we are being attacked by terrorists.

That is, what they themselves do with all sorts of atrocities against all of humanity, they assume that others do against their own people.

Due to obvious existing mental disorders due to historical persecution, they see terrible shadows of threats everywhere and everywhere, so it costs them nothing to kill an infant or a small child, assuming that he or she is a possible future terrorist.

It's not even worth mentioning older teenagers and adults; they're supposedly preoccupied with nothing but thinking about how to commit a terrorist attack. Therefore, due to their inner fears and obvious mental health issues, they naturally enjoy writing libelous remarks and especially denunciations.

I personally had the opportunity to become familiar with the texts of thousands of denunciations from representatives of all nations and hundreds of Jewish denunciations, starting from the Cheka, OGPU, NKVD, NKGB, MGB, and KGB.

If we take a proportional view, then more than half of all the many millions of denunciations over decades of Soviet rule were written by

Jews. Such a high level of creativity, with such content, clearly indicates an existing hereditary phenomenon—a mental disorder, in my opinion. This is an unusual fact, you'll agree, but how else can it be explained?

Given their habit of embellishing to maximize profits and downplaying their own shortcomings and guilt, as well as their manic passion for instantly shifting into positions of collective defense or attack, it is not surprising that the phenomenon of Zionism, through usury, usurping the media, penetrating the elites of many developed countries through the connections of financial magnates through corruption, and from there creating powerful lobby funds in parliaments and governments, managed to proclaim and accept into the public consciousness incorrect, contradictory, illogical concepts such as anti-Semitism and the Holocaust.

Here, on my part, there is no denial of such concepts, but they should be expanded to other Semitic peoples: Arabs (Algerians, Moroccans, Syrians, Lebanese, Libyans, Iraqis - their civilian population was killed without any reason by many millions of Europeans and the USA), which, by many indications, is a real Genocide.

The Holocaust is being experienced under total occupation by the innocently guilty Palestinian people, who have been experiencing an inhumane Genocide for many decades simply because the world community decided so (supposedly for free) for humanitarian reasons.

According to the most crude estimates, the spread of information on the number of people who died in concentration camps varies greatly, putting the figure at around 11 million. And this figure is among the 15 to 20 million people who, according to various estimates, passed through this system, primarily from the Soviet Union, whom the Nazis particularly hated.

Therefore, it's impossible to say with certainty that the Nazis would have been able to kill six million Jews out of that total. It's physically impossible; even the figure of three million seems difficult to achieve given the capabilities of Nazi Germany. But Jews insist on six million deaths in the Holocaust, and even consider this figure to be underestimated. It's terrifying to talk about, but why do scholars avoid discussing this topic?

The exact number of those killed in the excruciating, inhumane conditions cannot be determined due to the chaotic nature of the repeated information, seemingly deliberately mixed archival information, and some archives were destroyed and damaged during the war.

There was also a general mortality rate, with prisoners dying from hunger, disease, internal conflict, and forced labor. Because Zionists everywhere imposed a profound taboo on this issue, anyone who dared to express dissent would face far greater problems than Mel Gibson.

It is assumed that, according to statistics, 16.6 million Jews lived worldwide in 1940, and by 1948, approximately 11.5 million. This decline is explained by the massive losses incurred during the Holocaust. However, this ignores the fact that during the persecutions, hundreds of thousands of Jewish families, using their connections and financial resources, were forced, for objective reasons, to obtain new passports when changing their citizenship, surnames, and nationalities.

Basically, the Nazis focused all their efforts (to intimidate and minimize resistance) on excruciating torture, inhumane conditions of detention, abuse, and the murder of several million people, precisely those who put up worthy resistance—primarily Poles, Russians, Ukrainians, Belarusians, Balkan peoples, and the republics of the Soviet Union. If we apply logic and statistics and constructively relate everything to the events of that time, taking into account the number of people living and the possible number of people arriving in that time and place, the mythical Armenian Genocide also disappears . If we follow such an impartial and constructive approach, the myths of the supposedly voluntary annexation of Slavic principalities and Baltic peoples to the Moscow Prince, enslaved by the Golden Horde. Then, as Tsar of the principalities of the peoples of the Caucasus, the Khanates in Siberia and Central Asia with their thousand-year-old culture, and many other peoples and nationalities, will also disappear. The question of why and for what purpose this annexation was made is still not considered in the minds of the occupiers.

The Holodomor, the blatant genocide of the Ukrainian nation of 1932–1933, was orchestrated by a Zionist clique within the Soviet Union's leadership. Stalin was undoubtedly implicated for his non-intervention. Demographers estimate excess mortality in the Ukrainian SSR at between 2.6 and 3.9 million. Driven mad by hunger, Ukrainians ate everything they could digest; there were mass cases of cannibalism, and approximately two thousand cases were opened on such charges. The main organizers and perpetrators were V. Molotov, L. Kaganovich, M. Khatayevich , P. Postyshev, and S. Kosior —basically, they were the majority. Take S. Kosior , an ethnic Pole, who was completely unarmed by Jewish tactics, although he fought as best he could from the very beginning of his political career. He was manipulated like a puppet by Lazar Kaganovich and Mendel Khatayevich .

Key moments. On February 1, 1932, S. Kosior, General Secretary of the Central Committee of the Communist Party (Bolsheviks), and V. Chubar, Chairman of the Council of People's Commissars of the Ukrainian SSR, signed the decree "On Seeds," instructing local committees to deny seed aid to Ukrainian collective farms. On March 17, 1932, S. Kosior signed the decree "On Seed Reserves," which led to increased repression against peasants resisting the confiscation of grain. On March 29, they signed the decree "On Poliesia," according to which 500 peasant families were deported from the Poliesia region of Ukraine as an act of intimidation.

In April 1932, S.V. Kosior sent a telegram to I. Stalin :

"We have isolated cases and even individual villages of starving people, but this is only the result of local ineptitude and excesses, especially in relation to collective farms. Any talk of a 'famine' in Ukraine must be categorically rejected. The significant aid provided to Ukraine gives us the opportunity to eliminate all such outbreaks."

I. Stalin writes in a coded message to Lazar Kaganovich and Vyacheslav Molotov on July 2, 1932.

"Pay the utmost attention to Ukraine. Chubar, with his decay and opportunistic nature, and Kosior, with his rotten diplomacy (in relation to the Central Committee of the All-Union Communist Party) and criminally frivolous attitude, will completely ruin Ukraine. These comrades are not up to leading today's Ukraine. I have the impression (perhaps even the conviction) that both Chubar and Kosior will have to be removed from Ukraine. I may be wrong. But you will have the opportunity to verify this at the conference."

Between 1925 and 1939, a voluntary-forced migration was carried out from Kazakhstan by Zionists and Russian nationalists, as a result of which more than two million people, mainly Kazakhs and Uzbeks, were forced by circumstances of artificially created conditions to migrate, mainly to Siberia, the Uzbek SSR, and also migrated to China, Iran, Afghanistan, and Turkey.

In the Soviet era, the " Asharshilyk " (Holodomor) is considered part of the all-Union famine of 1932-1933, similar to the one in Ukraine, caused by the official policy of "destroying the kulaks as a class," collectivization, increasing food procurement quotas by the central government, and the de facto confiscation of livestock. Numerous cases of cannibalism were recorded during the famine. According to official statistics, approximately 1.5–2.3 million people, mostly Kazakhs, died of starvation. Without assistance from the semi-nomadic Uzbeks and Kyrgyz living in the south, who provided invaluable assistance in overcoming inhumane conditions through joint efforts, many more would have perished. Based on statistical and demographic facts, it is possible to estimate that far more than 3 million Kazakhs perished.

The main organizers of the famine were the Zionists who wrote directives with instructions for the application of methods of gradual collectivization and the departure of the indigenous population from the nomadic way of life, and demands to create more points for slaughtering cattle in the open steppe.

At each slaughterhouse, 500 to 1,000 sheep and 200 to 400 cows were slaughtered daily. However, the Freemasons failed to realize that, due to inadequate storage and transportation facilities, enormous quantities of meat were wasted and rotting, spreading disease. Based on many factors, it can be concluded that much was done deliberately to reduce the numbers of the indigenous population, which was clearly unsuitable for atheistic reforms.

In practice, those guilty of the Holodomor can be considered to be Filipp Isayevich Goloshchekin (real name Shaya Itsikovich), a homosexual, one of the organizers of the execution of the royal family, especially A. Mikoyan, also V. Molotov, L. Kaganovich, and certainly I. Stalin , who had full information about the cause of the Holodomor.

The Kazakh population from 1926, which numbered 3.62 million people, was reduced to 2.31 million people in 1939 , and this is taking into account that more than 400-500 thousand people were registered as Kazakhs, mainly Kalmyks, Tatars, Uzbeks, and Kyrgyz.

At the same time, the authorities increased the number of other ethnic groups by 3 million, displaced primarily from Russia, and some from Ukraine. To eliminate the strong influence of Islam among the people, it was decided to change the composition of the sedentary, nomadic, and semi-nomadic lifestyle of the indigenous population. This was genocide.

Now let's just note that it is customary to speak of two waves of repression: 1933-1934 and 1937-1938. The main culprits were I. Stalin and L. Beria.

I beg to differ, because in 1989–1990, the authorities had not yet managed to suppress the legacy of Mikhail Gorbachev's Glasnost. I spent a long time pondering the question: how and why did the repressions continue without interruption? People suspected of some terrible accusations, many war heroes, party workers, and scientists, suddenly, inexplicably, incriminated themselves and their loved ones during their very first interrogation.

Investigators churned out treason cases by the thousands, moving like a conveyor belt all the way to the troika court. There, the death penalty was already in effect, and those who received long sentences followed by exile to the wilderness were rarely lucky.

What was most surprising was that the majority of the authors of letters to the OGPU and NKVD accusing them of treason, betrayal, and harm caused to the Soviet people and government were Jews.

The investigators, operatives, interrogators, and chiefs throughout the hierarchy of the security agencies were mostly Jews.

The prosecutor's supervisory bodies were almost all made up of the same people, and they found virtually no violations in the charges, with rare exceptions when there were instructions from the Kremlin.

Also, for some reason, the Troikas of Judges were mainly composed of Jews.

Still, if we speak in essence, the repressions were carried out by Jews, the record holders: the Kaganovich brothers, wrote a huge number of valuable instructions in their speeches at various plenary sessions, emergency meetings, radio broadcasts, Yuli Kaganovich, who was especially distinguished, was part of the special troika of the NKVD.

Vyacheslav Molotov, G. Yagoda (Genakh Gershenovich, one of the main leaders of the security agencies of the Cheka, GPU, OGPU, NKVD), Lev Mekhlis (a man with an unstable psyche, from 1930 to 1937 the head of the press department of the Central Committee of the party, then the editor-in-chief of the newspaper Pravda, wrote countless articles demanding an intensification of the fight against the "enemies of the people", twice allowed himself to attack members of the Politburo/Stalin/, that they, while valuing the old merits of rotten comrades, do not fight enough to expose conspiracies and entrenched spies).

Of course, the following are guilty: I. Stalin (General Secretary of the Central Committee of the All-Union Communist Party (Bolsheviks), Zhdanov, Voroshilov, Malenkov, Beria, of course Khryushchev and thousands of other murderers .

There have been similar scenarios of discrimination around the world for racial and other reasons.

Nearly 4 million Indians died in the 1943–1944 famine created by Winston Churchill's government in Bengal, British India. This Holodomor was described by contemporaries as "the greatest catastrophe on the subcontinent in the 20th century."

The celebrated Prime Minister's utterances remain: "I hate Hindus. They are a brutal people with a brutal religion." Also, in response to the Bengal administration's desperate pleas for emergency food supplies, Churchill, enraged, went so far as to blame the Indians themselves for the famine, loudly declaring that Indians were "breeding like rabbits."

It seems that such unpleasant, acute problematic research and questions, which still leave residual traces and influence the relations between peoples, should be dealt with primarily by scientists from these ethnic groups and peoples, in order to reach a consensus and reconciliation through mutual concessions.

People of the world must not forget that we are the descendants of the forefather prophet Adam and the foremother Chava (Eve), and therefore any labels with claims to racial, ethnic, national superiority, God's chosenness and greatness are unacceptable.

In Islam, this is explained as follows: Allah the Most High, the Holy and Great, sent Messengers and prophets to the peoples with teachings in the Books, and also divided them into nations so that people, like brothers, would show which religion and nation are better in worship and the fulfillment of divine commandments.

The division into nations and tribes was intended to enable people to recognize one another, not to create barriers to prevent communication. The primary characteristic of a person in Islam is fear of God. The teachings testify that the most revered person before Allah is not the one who belongs to a particular faith or nation, but the one who fears God most.

The Islamic worldview contains a covenant—a call for unity. All views, ideas, and thoughts must strive for maturity on the path to a universal, perfect unity. The idea of separation between peoples and religions is used to call for understanding and strengthening of faith, rather than confrontation.

The Jews are characterized by their clannish nature and the transmission of their ethnicity through the maternal line. Whatever it may be, everything exists and develops within a strict, closed clan system. They won't let others get close, for from birth they've lived by the idea of "us and against everyone."

All other peoples develop patriarchally, preserving the family structure, the dynastic type, the familial one. Everything is open and visible. For centuries, They have exploited this, selecting the best of the best, giving them daughters, or hooking up an extra carriage to a train at their own expense and collecting all the valuable essence they needed. Therefore, They have the advantage.

In 1903, the Jewish diaspora itself seriously considered the possibility of establishing a New Israel in Argentina. But at the same time, through various means, they quietly created a cozy Israel for themselves in the United States, where approximately three million Jews emigrated between 1870 and 1942.

Between 1870 and 1914, approximately 2 million Jews arrived in the United States from the Russian Empire alone. By 1939, the Jewish population was approximately 4.5 million, or 3.7% of the country's population. They immediately assumed leading positions in the media, trade, stock exchanges, financial speculation, banking, pawnshops, casinos, illegal liquor sales, drug trafficking, prostitution, fraud, and established a strong presence in the criminal underworld.

The immigrants created a powerful Zionist movement in all spheres of public activity; clannishness allowed them to constantly move and invest their collective capital in various profitable projects, as information flowed from everywhere to their leaders like a spider's web. With the help of this, by the second or third decade of the 20th century, they founded the most economically powerful political lobby in the US Congress, and today it is they who have achieved power in all branches of US government.

Let us return to the time of the creation of the World Jewish Congress, to the era when arrogant upstarts, ambitious young Anglo-Saxon aristocrats wanted not only to rule, but also to manipulate the Jews as puppets.

Meanwhile, painstaking work was underway in all three factions of world Jewry. In Polotsk, they discovered a notorious fanatical Zionist patriot who, by reading many volumes of old, secular books, had made significant progress in studying the forgotten Hebrew language in its new edition—a certain Eliezer ben Yehuda . This man displayed resourcefulness, coming up with nearly a thousand words to connect concepts, enough to make it possible, according to the concept of the revival, to study Hebrew in higher religious educational institutions, such as yeshivas .

At the same time, students could conduct language courses in their families.

of the Messiah was launched into the dense, twilight consciousness of the chosen people .

Mass psychosis infected the riotous consciousness of this perpetually persecuted, deluded people. In several countries, authorities struggled to quell outbursts of popular anger over the ritual murders of teenagers, which could have escalated into pogroms and lynchings. The revival of Hebrew became a reality, offering enormous opportunities for espionage and the creation of agent networks across the globe, especially in the Anglo-Saxon territories of the United States and Great Britain.

These factions were constantly relentlessly perfecting their secret methods for engaging civil servants, judges, prosecutors, ambassadors, and army generals in corruption. The need to revive the lost language was strongly supported, and sponsors allocated vast sums of money. But these stipends, of course, never reached ordinary, poor families with many children, barely making ends meet. They, as always, found themselves stuck between rabbis, banks, and a multitude of secret cells, resembling sects, where they trained propagandists, spies, swindlers, murderers, and prostitutes.

CHAPTER 2

White light is needed above you,

Your life with me is legal.

Let us not be in this world,

Reader, do not sadden the world with your darkness.

Christianity is a world religion for those who believe only in the Law of God with the addition of the Trinity. Simply put, it is a religion based on faith: God the Father in heaven, the Holy Spirit descending upon the Virgin Mary, who later became the Mother of God, and Jesus Christ as the Son of God. The Messiah, prophesied in the Old Testament, atoned for the sin of Adam and Eve by his sacrifice on the cross and freed humanity from original sin, and his life, death, and resurrection atoned for the future sins of Christians alone. This sacrifice, according to Christian teaching, brings eternal life and salvation only to those who believe in Jesus Christ as God in human form.

A convenient religion and surprisingly tempting. Fishermen lure fish into their nets, saying, "Catch a fish, big or small." Supposedly, the Son of God, by his death on the cross, atoned for all the sins of mankind, and now they can sin without rest, left and right... Just make sure you cross yourself; there's an indulgence for all time.

These definitions were conveyed to me back in 1990 by Rabbi David in Budapest, where we arrived as part of a delegation of USSR cooperators to share experiences in the agricultural sector, development and cooperation in the agro-industrial sector.

It is believed that Valentine's Day, celebrated on February 14th, has been celebrated in the United States, as well as around the world, since 1777. However, the brownie Oceanarim claims that Michael Bloomberg, now mayor of New York City, added the "spiritual spice" to this sweet, heart-shaped chocolate, as he was born on this day, which is why it has become so celebrated in this metropolis.

All churches—the Catholic Church, the Anglican Communion, Eastern Orthodoxy, and Lutheranism—venerate Saint Valentine, primarily in the person of the Martyr Bishop of Terni. However, due to the many versions and disagreements, the image of this martyr is blurred, and there are many versions.

Today, this holiday is celebrated by the worshippers of Sodom and Gomorrah, and is of interest and profit only to the Zionists, who, with the help of this highly dubious holiday, are nullifying the laws of the Christian religion.

Already, at the end of 2006, the world's national security agencies, Interpol, and other special anti-corruption agencies of independent countries must begin joint preparatory work to prevent future fraudulent schemes and operations. High-level hackers, specially trained by Zionists, will soon begin to operate, launching their dizzying money-making schemes into the information space without leaving home, offering extremely profitable fraudulent operations.

Sleeper agencies are training specialists to rob the gullible population by creating criminal communities online and on social media. With all sorts of enticing advertisements about profitable investments on social media, they're already training money-making experts in St. Petersburg, and I'd like to point out that the vast majority of them are Jewish. I've personally met with them and discussed many things. They openly paint a picture of future success in public, talking about the prospects for easy enrichment that await them, and revealing secrets about how they communicate with like-minded individuals in

Israel, the United States, and around the world using methods known only to them, sharing their know-how and experience.

Global law enforcement agencies are already significantly behind in terms of computer intelligence skills and competence to be able to suppress the activities of criminal organizations.

The internet and social media could fall into Zionist hands, just like the media, banks, the judicial system, and governments. This is extremely dangerous. The emerging cadres, composed of representatives of various nationalities, will serve their masters, just as they are now doing at the next table. Beautiful young people, most of them slender and athletic, but all subservient to two stooped, snot-nosed bespectacled men who, with their noses in their mouths, allow themselves to be rude to them in public.

And I think the internet will be a great disaster for the world's population. They will spread obscenities, vileness, and filth, while the rest of the planet's population, represented by the majority of people, will, like useful idiots, amuse themselves in this filthy cesspool and slap each other with disgusting blasphemy.

The pleasures of entertainment for those obsessed with sexual passions will end with the loss of valuable money. Then begins a protracted struggle of "denigrating the other side," wild interethnic squabbles with or without cause, fortunately, history has accumulated many problems.

A tug-of-war between historical issues will begin in millions of video and audio releases by the creative intelligentsia, as well as by intriguers of various specialties, essentially ignorant of matters of history, jurisprudence, and so on, who nevertheless actively participate in the brawl. Everything will benefit the Zionists, including financially.

If a local war breaks out somewhere on this soil, it will also turn out to be to their advantage. They are already preparing to openly engage in a fight with the rest of the world, not for life , but for death. The rest of humanity walks around sleepily, seeing nothing but their own personal needs and problems, everyone is consumed by everyday life.

They've cultivated a consumerist, dull-witted society ignorant of religion, history, and legal matters, and now they're just ripping it off. Every single well-known food, beverage, and alcohol brand, every company in every sphere of human needs, social life, and communications, they hold a controlling stake... But even that, it seems, isn't enough for them.

"However, perhaps this will save humanity from their centuries-long enslavement? They have occupied all the peoples of the world, enslaving their freethinking with all sorts of passions. They have crammed psychoanalytic concepts into school curricula and are already destroying the brains of the younger generation from the school bench."

Muslims resist this total systemic pressure . They don't hang out at night in Satanist establishments, don't drink wine, don't use drugs, don't use prostitutes, don't take out loans with interest, don't raise the next generation in an immoral manner, but rather engage in God-pleasing activities, dedicate their free time to studying monotheism, pray, and care for the chastity of society.

And all this irritates and angers the Zionists, who are forced to corrupt the hearts and souls of people who, for some unknown reason, consider themselves Christians with vile images. These naive people begin to act thoughtlessly but decisively against these potentially dangerous so-called Islamists. When will this collective hypnosis end? Probably only when science recognizes the concept of psychoanalysis as a fraud. I predict that it will be Christians who will resist this total pressure and destroy the Zionists.

Soon, and it's not far off, the internet, along with social media, will acquire enormous powers to manipulate public opinion. This will further enhance Zionism's treasury with enormous opportunities to prepare adults around the world—most of whom are literate, educated, and knowledgeable—to voluntarily part with their personal savings, without any major investment of energy, time, or money.

And this will inevitably happen. It will be so. The ignorant demand bread and circuses, and they don't need the constraints of culture. There will be fistfights inside cages for money, and blood will be spilled on the battlefield over online comments, for as Al-Farabi famously said, "enslavement to one's passions is the most terrible slavery."

- Does anyone doubt it? Good.

Let us remember the Covenant of the Prophet Musa (Moses) that he made with Allah Almighty when God chose them as his people.

They were delivered from slavery by the Egyptians in a miraculous way.

God fed them with the best food, manna from heaven and quails, for forty years, but they still did not fully believe in the Omnipotence of Elohim.

When they gained knowledge about God and the rules of life in the Law of the Most High Creator, reflecting in the endless desert, understanding the meaning of freedom in two generations under the leadership of the Prophet and Messenger Musa, peace and blessings of Allah be upon him, they still did not get rid of the treachery of doubt.

The blessing from the Most High Allah was immeasurable and generous; they only needed to conquer their hearts with the fear of God, cleanse their minds and souls from all filth and doubts, submit completely to the divine Law and call upon other peoples to honor God and fulfill the basic truths.

But for forty years they hid sin within themselves, and nurtured vengeful feelings in their minds, hiding their sinful essence in their lost souls by hiding the gold they had stolen from the Egyptians.

And the people of Israel have committed countless abominations and will commit more, for they have not repented. The Torah of Moses clearly and truthfully reveals everything. God chose this people specifically to demonstrate the folly of self-interest and unbelief, with its treachery, in all its glory.

The Great Prophet Musa, the Messenger of Allah Almighty, brother of the Prophet Harun (Aaron) and descendant of the Prophet Yaqub (Jacob), peace and blessings be upon the prophets, called his people to reverence and humble awe before the Greatness of Allah Almighty and ascended Mount Sinai to receive the Law.

As soon as he left his people, grumbling and discontent began.

And the people of Israel committed abominations and blasphemy of such a horrific nature, and, in fact, immeasurable in their blasphemy. They violated the Covenant made by Prophet Musa with the Most High God, Holy and Great is He.

From the gold stolen from the Egyptians during the Exodus, which they hid from the leaders of the brothers of the prophets for two generations and forty years, the blasphemers created the Golden Calf and worshiped it, thereby betraying the mission of the prophets.

Also, according to the Treaty given by the promise of the Prophet Musa, they, having cleansed themselves of filth and having completely trusted in the Omnipotence of the Most High God, were to enter the Holy Land of Canaan, kneeling with honey and an olive branch...

They entered with outrageous greed to the hospitable, peaceful, God-fearing people of the Philistines , who never shed blood, who lived only by prayers, caring for the graves of the prophets, and by the alms of travelers and pilgrims, whom they met, showing honor and respect, welcoming them with shelter, bread, and salt...

They entered with fire and sword, brutally slaughtering all civilians, men and women, old and children, including the cattle, not sparing even the donkeys. They spared only a few thousand virgin children for the amusement of their heroes and leaders. They had intercourse with them from the age of three.

In Moscow, legends were created about heroes of "backbreaking labor swindlers," Jewish swindlers, bandits, and army cadres from military academies with criminal pasts who, after confessing to crimes committed and signing a pledge to cooperate with the KGB, were sent with the task of finding the best possible permanent residence in the United States in order to provide assistance and help in the future to "people needed by the fatherland."

Well, it is a well-known fact that 99.99% of those who emigrated from the USSR to the USA with a higher education were initially recruited by the SVR of the First Main Directorate, while the majority of the older generation completed the necessary courses on how to quickly get in touch with an urgent message in case of need.

The whole of Brighton Beach is heart and soul devoted to Israel and the Kremlin, though sometimes the two sides trade places. The KGB didn't recruit as many valuable agents as the émigrés managed to lure spies to their side. They even managed to lure a possible future American President to the Soviet ambassador in late 1986.

Of course, at the dinner party, this chatterbox, not particularly distinguished in manners or intellect, boasting of his connections and opportunities, was appreciated, especially in terms of the financial problems this supposed businessman was facing, including the threat of bankruptcy.

But the Soviets had money in such huge quantities that they could afford the unthinkable: to spend billions in such a primitive, careless manner on countries with an orientation toward socialism, in order to allegedly harm world imperialism.

History will write it off, and descendants will forgive it , the current Kremlin inmate likes to repeat.

So here's the rest of the story. The important thing here isn't whether this project will come to fruition or not.

On some entertainment program on central television, famous people invited onto the air, all of them Jews, were openly discussing the world's agenda: politicians Primakov, Yavlinsky, Nemtsov, and Zhirinovsky; bankers Fridman, Aven, and Smolensky, also Jews; media owners Berezovsky and Gusinsky; and the richest of them all, Khodorkovsky. Again, the power of the elites, of whom, as always, there's no need to list them. And this is Russia's elite.

So, of course, they were already gradually filtering their speeches. Yeltsin was clearly no longer physically capable of governing and was speaking frankly about a successor. The conversation suddenly took a sharp turn from domestic issues to foreign ones, and they, at first jokingly, then in all seriousness, with omissions and hints, began discussing how many presidential candidates the KGB had managed to prepare around the world.

Primakov or Burbulis hinted that on a summer night in 1987, the long-legged Senior Lieutenant Maslova managed to recruit a master of business deals within two hours. True, this mythical tycoon of unprofitable businesses was promised financial assistance worth several hundred million. And yet, no one in that taiga kibbutz was laughing or joking anymore.

Then they named the names of people, not yet widely known, capable of acting in the Kremlin's interests in South America, Europe, Asia, and Africa. They became so enthusiastic about listing their existing capabilities that someone even claimed that the KGB, in its heyday, was far weaker than the trump cards they now hold, gained primarily from oil and gas sales.

At the same time, they no longer spoke on behalf of the Kremlin, the Ministry of Defense, the FSB, the FSK, and the GRU; they clearly meant themselves as influential Zionists.

Emigrants from Odessa, the Caucasus, Bukhara, New York and other US cities have particularly demonstrated their criminal abilities.

Unwashed Brighton Beach is, of course, famous for its comical, artistic mafiosi and pot-bellied prostitutes, who fleeced the treasury and the citizens of the enemy empire as best they could, because circumstances allowed it. They know how to joke about anything, like, "He who doesn't work must eat well to look respectable." They came up with such types of businesses: cutting gasoline, bottling alcohol in Brooklyn basements, shady tenders for repair and construction projects, laying and repairing asphalt, hundreds of types of insurance fraud, money laundering, banking fraud, obtaining loans through fictitious persons, pharmacy fraud, car accidents with and without passengers, with subsequent assessments in their auto repair stations, mass openings of shady offices: doctors, physical therapists, dentists, caregivers for the elderly, children, the disabled and the sick - theater and circus everywhere, all amateur artists, and all out of interest.

Corruption can also occur in restaurants, with the help of waiters. A mosquito wouldn't scratch its nose. This merry-go-round is a joyride of ingenuity and hypocrisy.

In such a turbulent climate of passions and activity, blinded by the financial flows of Zionist corruption, one can expect major upheavals soon. When they live happily, a vital effect immediately begins to boil within them.

They are everywhere, in all forms of media, which are completely like hostages in their clammy hands, beginning to carry out all sorts of diversionary maneuvers, so that nowhere is there talk about the vile crimes committed specifically by the Jews with the mass murder of people on ethnic and religious grounds, which abound in all sacred scriptures, which are recorded in all parts of the world, of course, also especially registered by international observers as horrific atrocities against the indigenous inhabitants of the Holy Land, the Palestinian people, from 1948 to the present day.

And what makes this abomination even worse is the fact that Palestinians are closely related to Jews. Let's briefly review the precedent.

Prophet Ishmael was the eldest son of Prophet Ibrahim (Abraham), and is said to be the father of the Arabs. Prophet Ishaq (Isaac) was the second son of Prophet Ibrahim (Abraham), and is said to be the father of many Semitic peoples. His eldest son, Esau, is said to be the father of the Assyrians, Palestinians, Lebanese, Maltese, and others. The Jews are said to be the descendants of Jacob, the youngest son, who, in a parable in the Torah, on the advice of his mother, deceitfully exchanged his elder brother Esau for a bowl of lentil stew, and then, using his father's poor eyesight to deceive him into giving him a blessing instead of Esau.

But let us stipulate that the truth is known only to Allah Almighty.

Jews have never lived well, and there's no point in trying to start one. Prosperity in one or two generations always breeds intellectual ferment. Soon, the phenomenon of hysteria appears, and here and there, talk of the coming of another Moshiach is heard . Somehow, in the dark corridors of synagogues, in the corridors of gloomy basements and dungeons, in the secret whispers of gossip and rumors, a cunning selection takes place for the most suitable to fulfill the role of Rebbe. Preferably, an elderly fanatic, able to speak in several languages, the crooked ornaments of correct formulas about world Jewry, all sorts of incomprehensible taiga nonsense, and, most importantly, while counting banknotes with a wet finger, prophesying the coming of Moshiach .

From here, it's a short step to creating artificial hotbeds of tension, masterfully orchestrated by the media in long-running disputes between naive and trusting neighbors. The catalyst, like a spark in an explosive situation, is in their hands and can be launched at any time, like a bowling ball, to spark numerous wars and bloody military conflicts around the world.

The arms trade will begin, and this must be sanctified by the ritual sacrifice of the blood of a Christian child, followed by the burning of the bones to appease Milk. The sale of ships, planes, tanks, missile systems, lethal weapons, and ammunition. The sale of emergency food supplies, whose shelf life is shortening. Secret design bureaus begin working to create newer types of weapons using the latest technology, and factories commissioned by the Ministry of Defense begin working three shifts. They act as a link everywhere.

Anti-Semitism, as an existing concept misconstrued in the media, as an absurd phenomenon, requires rethinking and reformatting, with mandatory subsequent restitution of all capital undeservedly acquired through the vile exploitation of this idea, for subsequent proper distribution. This would be logical and fair. Most importantly, it is the Jews who terrorize, systematically and systematically destroy, and commit violence against the Semites of the Middle East, while simultaneously using their agents in the media to demonize the defenseless, occupied indigenous population.

In essence, Israel, through the promotion of this contradictory false concept of Anti-Semitism, has turned all the neighboring countries of the region, and in particular the long-suffering Palestinian people, into whipping boys.

And what is most strange here is that Israel, created by the UN, completely ignores all the adopted Resolutions of this same international body, taking advantage of the presence of powerful Zionists in the Parliaments and Governments of influential countries of the world.

But this does not evoke any emotions in any of them; everyone has forgotten about it for more than half a century now.

Why does this happen? Isn't it simply because they're deliberately increasing the number of people who might be subjected to unfair, hostile, and humiliating treatment?

Approximately half a billion people in the world are Semitic. However, the only people benefiting from this have been Jews for over a hundred years.

And let's take into account the important fact that, according to statistics, there were only about fourteen million of them in the world at the end of 2006. That is, all the benefits of the Prevost over the simple rights of other nations and peoples in the UN, from these adopted laws and obligations in all countries of the world, with respect to approximately half a billion people, are used and openly received by only 14 million. This is undoubtedly the scam of the century. And here we should also consider the important argument that all educated people in the world know and understand that there are at least three times as many Jews.

They live as highly professional spy agents among other nations and peoples, changing their ethnicity, names and surnames.

This is not a joke, but a rather dangerous problem, which is growing every year in terms of the volume of dangers for 7.5 billion goyim in various planes of manifestation.

These thirty million are under the watchful eye of fourteen million officially recognized Sacred Cows with enhanced civil rights, who are on the lookout among them for the smart, the cunning, the treacherous, the ruthless, and they all have self-interest.

These currents circulate organically and continuously within the interconnected vessels of a single, shared organism, painstakingly maintaining the intensity of passions at the required level. Sometimes raising, sometimes lowering, releasing a threatening steam as a warning signal, perhaps by killing a politician, a journalist, or even a veteran fascist who escaped conviction and punishment, with the help of the secret services, allegedly for his criminal past, by committing an act of murder in another country.

And, mind you, everything always goes unpunished. Countries where such public acts of execution and murder occur calmly wipe away the stinking stain on their sovereignty and independence without indignation.

especially barbaric when the occupiers, using special harassment techniques to provoke the psyche of a chosen victim—some unstable Palestinian in, say, Jerusalem or Gaza—so that at some point he will succumb to the pressure and take up a knife, a gun, or a cobblestone for revenge, or arrest without charge any passerby allegedly suspected of terrorism, including a child.

"Who's going to sort this out?" "Who needs it? Could any well-fed European or American possibly believe that such sweet-looking, timid, and hesitant Jews, wearing glasses and holding a violin, are capable of not only smashing a child's head against a wall, but even verbally insulting him? Let alone think about the centuries-old ritual traditions of sacrificing Christian children to Milk... Besides, they have an interest, too.

How many secrets about ritual sacrifices are hidden in the metropolis of New York and the state of New Jersey?

Conspiracy theories, hysteria, the ravings of a madman, or the fantasies of a half-wit, might be the thought of a modern, supposedly sober-minded layman, usually capable of thinking with his stomach, and only when the mood strikes.

But why and for what purpose in Manhattan and elsewhere are there mysterious structures and buildings of unusual design, framed on all sides by magical Masonic and other pagan symbols, and also equipped with the best security and video surveillance systems?

Moreover, it is probably no coincidence that they are surrounded by high iron fences and massive entrance doors, so that even with a strong desire it will be difficult for a police squad to penetrate them in the event of an emergency.

As can be seen from the outside, judging by the fact that these strange facilities are rarely cleaned, and especially at the entrance areas, alarming thoughts arise.

"Who needs to maintain such exotic buildings in Manhattan, with their unclear intended purpose and, what's more, extremely expensive to maintain? Furthermore, this suggests that all these entrance and exit openings are clearly decorative, and that there are other underground utilities hidden from view or secret passages through corridors from other nearby buildings."

And these circumstances, apparently, are of little concern or interest to the Federal special services, state and municipal police. - Why?

In all of this, it's clear that there are exceptions to the general rules for everyone else—that is, the paradox of double standards is obvious. There are many of them, and the same thing exists to a slightly lesser extent in other countries.

All sorts of scams and adventures are devised in unprincipled secret societies and brought to life in the Zionist Lobbies, which openly meet in the Great Powers and most of the developed countries of the world, certainly in the G20.

And no one in the global media seems bothered by this. They're particularly concerned and worried by the fact that more and more people are embracing Islam with their hearts and souls every day, and, of course, by the mythical so-called Islamic terrorism, invented, no one knows where and why.

If even a seasoned politician or journalist, even one who had achieved universal recognition, had addressed humanity with these words: Friends! Islam is, it turns out, a religion of goodness and peace! Educate yourself, read the divine Quran. Here Allah says that the murder of one innocent person is tantamount to the murder of all humanity. The Almighty God commands: there is no compulsion in faith. Believe me, I assure you, this great lover of truth would not have lived long. Either he would have suffered a terrible embarrassment, been caught with a bribe, or suddenly, in a fit of delirium, committed a crime.

In all Christian countries, Israeli citizens are always in positions of power. They always have a fund, called an electoral fund, into which funds are deposited.

The question is, where do they come from?

It's all official; all the so-called Great Countries have been paying tribute from the taxes of their citizens since the 1940s.

Enormous sums flow into the Holy Land, and then half of this jackpot returns back to the accounts of the Zionists' election funds, at the disposal of the Lobby elite so that they can occasionally grease the millstones of the corrupt machine, maintain a large staff of service personnel: candidates for various levels of power, volunteers, celebrities, journalists, prostitutes, killers, their loyal servants in the courts, prosecutors' offices, law enforcement agencies, and special services.

Over more than half a century of experience, this mechanism has come to work precisely, almost like a clock...

Of the remaining half, the lion's share goes to the secret managers from among the most influential individuals, who use it specifically for certain ready-made, pre-planned business projects, and also direct funds toward the purchase or construction of real estate in the USA and Europe, and the opening of Jewish centers, universities, colleges, schools, and kindergartens.

The remaining funds are subjected to extensive processing by statisticians, accountants, and economists to balance the books. Then, from this still-significant pile of money, the most influential figures in the Knesset and the Cabinet of Ministers nibble away chunks. These chunks are given to informal criminal organizations overseen by intelligence officials to carry out various operations to make life difficult for the indigenous Palestinian Arab population. Others are distributed to various non-governmental organizations and other social projects to assist newly arrived settlers, and so on.

We shouldn't forget about secret meetings in specially created clubs where sexual orgies with minors and ritual murders take place. Participation in such criminal activities fosters trust between participants and also definitely becomes a tool for blackmail.

Even of the remaining 7-8% of international aid, the spending and distribution of funds is carefully discussed with Hamas and representatives of the Palestinian Authority in the Gaza Strip and parts of the West Bank, most of whom are agents of Zionism and collaborators, but in public they play roles according to the Israeli scenario.

I've already given you some hints on many questions, including this one. Those who think will come up with answers, and those who reflect will find them. Those who doubt their own judgment can try to find partial answers from a knowledgeable Jew, an honest, conscientious, and seasoned moralist, Norman Filkelstein, in his book "The Holocaust Industry."

The Zionists in Europe and the US who have fared well are those who have found themselves at the forefront of politics, economics, science, and business, especially microbiology, computer programming, and artificial intelligence development. It is they who are now being infused with the legal resources and the seething energy of these far-flung forces within the sprawling Foundations.

Misfortune struck the indigenous inhabitants of the Holy Land, the Philistines, from an unexpected source. Not on May 17, 1948, when the USSR unexpectedly became the first of all to de jure recognize the State of Israel, nor did it arise decades earlier, when arriving refugees began periodically committing massacres of the local indigenous population under various pretexts. Rather, it came just over a hundred years ago, in 1840. In 1839, Abdulmejid I, a devout Muslim, a man of progressive views, exceptionally high spirituality, and an intellectual, became Sultan of the Ottoman Empire. Unfortunately for the Sultanate, the ruler was trusting of the advice of his sometimes less-than-selfless entourage, capable of implementing reforms while ignoring the compelling fact that there might not be enough personnel, both in quantity and quality, to successfully implement innovations and smoothly implement them.

The empire was clearly in a protracted decline due to financial problems, which undoubtedly didn't arise out of nowhere, especially when surrounded by enemies. Spies from powerful European powers literally infested the vast empire, like hyenas surrounding a wounded lion. Moreover, all sorts of political ideas, including atheistic thinking, were penetrating Turkey from Europe. Here, it's necessary to pause and clarify some important details of how events unfolded.

In 1839, Sultan Abdulmecid I signed a decree modernizing reforms in the Ottoman Empire, ushering in the Tanzimat (Regulation) era, which emphasized socioeconomic reforms rather than military reforms as had been common previously. The reforms were aimed at rapprochement with European powers by adapting the existing monarchy to the norms of Western European civilization. According to the plan of a group of educated bureaucrats led by Mustafa Rashid Pasha, these reforms were intended to strengthen the supreme authority of the sultan and his ministers and to weaken the development of national liberation movements in the vast multicultural empire.

Several years prior, events unfolded as follows. Accurate information from the archives of the chancellery of Ibrahim Pasha, the military commander of the Governor of Egypt, Muhammad Ali Pasha, as of September 11, 1833 AD: The population of Palestine was slightly over 292,000. Of these, the indigenous Philistines numbered approximately 270,000. Arabs numbered approximately 13,000.

Syrians and Lebanese numbered approximately 4,000. Jews (mostly Sephardim) numbered approximately 3,000. Armenians (with a small number of Georgians) numbered approximately 300. Turks of various nationalities numbered approximately 500. Pilgrims from all over the world numbered approximately 300. Representatives from Europe, including priests, numbered approximately 220. These reports also include representatives of the administration and military units protecting the Law.

It was during this period, from 1832 to 1840, that transformations took place, implemented by the new wave of Anglo-Saxon elites with the tacit consent of the Egyptians, who imitated the Europeans. They began to carry out editing under the guise of research in biblical history, geography, and archaeology. All in the name of profit, both monetary and political. The world had never seen so much replica tinted to look antique; prospectors everywhere attempted to create antique curiosities, and unique counterfeiters emerged.

In 1838, the Egyptian government, breaking a millennia-old taboo, suddenly allowed England to open a consulate in Beit al-Muqaddas (Jerusalem). Previously, Turkish authorities had only permitted European and Asian countries to open consulates and representative offices in the ports of Haifa, Acre, and Jaffa, to facilitate the travel of pilgrims from around the world.

This frivolous maneuver turned out to be the beginning of endless future upheavals with the turmoil of inhuman crimes, the boundless pain of the indigenous population of the Holy Land - the Philistines , the meek, hospitable, faithful, God-fearing people of Islam and the subsequent distortion of the facts of history in the name of the power of shameless embezzlers.

Zionism has always been a secret society of corrupt officials, the majority of whose members are usually boorish fanatics of a stupid idea, or useful idiots by chance, who also get crumbs from the bloody pie; in the minority are seasoned politicians, tricksters with unlimited possibilities, who have at their disposal a legally existing club of elite interests, which already exists in all developed countries.

In 1841, Syria and Palestine were returned to the direct control of the Ottoman Empire, as they had been since 1517, under Sultan Selim I. Reforms in Palestine paved the way for future upheavals among the indigenous Philistine population . By 1850, all major Christian European states—Catholics, Orthodox, Protestants—including the United States, had the right to open consular offices in Jerusalem. The wheel of troubles was set in motion; spies and military specialists were the first to arrive, and for some reason, all the representatives from various countries arriving were invariably Jews.

In 1841, Pope Gregory XVI established the Patriarchate, and in 1847, Pope Pius IX appointed the first Catholic Latin Patriarch of Jerusalem.

The oldest autocephalous local Orthodox Church has existed for centuries; it is the fourth in the diptych of autocephalous local churches. It is one of the five ancient patriarchates of the Ecumenical Church since 531. The Church is the oldest in the Christian world; it received the status of patriarchate at the Council of Chalcedon in 451.

In 1880, according to the census conducted by volunteers from among the Turkish pilgrims, the population of Palestine was as a whole with guests more than 450 thousand people, the indigenous inhabitants of the Philistines about 277 thousand people, the local settled population: Arabs 18 thousand people, all others 24 thousand people (of which 8 thousand Sephardic Jews, 1300 Ashkenazim, the rest Christians: Orthodox, Catholics, Protestants), all other representative bodies with their families, priests, travelers, military personnel, merchants, sailors, interpreters, doctors, etc.

Since the end of the 19th century, Western consular missions have acquired great importance in their countries, because for the opportunity to visit the Holy Land of Palestine, in particular the holy places of Jerusalem, travelers, pilgrims, and especially Jews, offered large sums of gold, silver, and jewelry.

The First Aliyah began in 1881, a large wave of Jewish immigration, when they were allegedly forced to flee pogroms in Eastern Europe. However, neither newspaper nor police records confirm this, yet these pogroms strangely exist and are described in Jewish history.

The Second Aliyah (1904–1914) began after the Kishinev pogrom. European officials who facilitated the resettlement of Jews to Palestine were able to rake in enormous sums of money in the form of exorbitant bribes. According to European statistics, documents for the two Aliyahs were issued for 50,000 people, but more than half of the refugees never reached the ports of Palestine. A terrible plague of hunger and cold also decimated the sick and exhausted, men, women, and children, and spared no one, not even the elderly.

I believe many special operations—pogroms, terrorist attacks, famines, especially those on a global scale—are carefully planned in advance, with precise calculations of how they might be used and ultimately to whose advantage. At the end of the operation, the beneficiaries are revealed. This operation, presented below, was clearly a trial run in its primitive planning, a terrifying provocation conceived by influential individuals within the Zionist hierarchy, with the clearly defined goal of causing panic among the Jewish diaspora, so that they would, without hesitation, frivolously, and out of self-preservation, agree to travel to an unknown Palestine with their families.

What is known about the Kishinev pogrom? Besides the fact that the most notorious pogrom in the Russian Empire occurred on April 6-7, 1903, in which 43 people were killed , 38 of whom were Jews. About five people were maimed, and 456 suffered minor injuries, 394 of whom were Jews. 1,351 buildings were damaged in the city, 75% of the victims were male, mostly adults, with rare exceptions. The police found no traces of torture. Three indictments for rape were filed. There is an isolated case of self-mutilation: a Jewish man, formerly blind in one eye, accuses a teenage neighbor of intentionally gouging out his other eye with a weight on a string, taking advantage of the confusion and general panic.

This is all about the results of the pogrom, according to Goremykin's prosecutorial report. The Jewish Congress, the European media, and Western governments, as if in concert, began to accuse the prosecutor of attempting to conceal the fact that the pogrom had been organized and the complicity of the Russian imperial authorities. They began talking about saving Jews.

Meanwhile, this is clearly slander. At the beginning of the century, the Jewish diaspora in the Russian Empire was one of the most influential in the power hierarchy in terms of total economic power. They were present in the banking and industrial sectors, were represented in all businesses, and were present at all levels of local government. Discriminatory rules against Jews (non-Christians) applied by the tsarist regime included restrictions on the right to reside in several major cities, which created obstacles to economic and social life. Consequently, many were forced to convert to Christianity and Orthodoxy. There were also restrictions on social status. Despite their leadership in economic achievement, most of the wealthiest Jewish bankers, moneylenders, and financial magnates faced enormous obstacles in attaining high government and political positions.

It is especially worth noting here that, by this time, over the past hundred years, there had been no manifestations of Judeophobia in the Russian Empire.

Based on this, neither the palace of the Emperor of the Russian Tsar nor the local authorities in Chisinau could have been interested in this tragedy for many reasons.

The famous financiers mentioned above may have been interested in this, as they paid the best newspaper journalists to trumpet all sorts of fabrications about the pogrom for weeks, exaggerating the number of victims. They also allocated all the sums due in various currencies to many European countries for the processing of documents, travel tickets for lists of people, provided food and other expenses, and quickly prepared ships to resettle thousands of people in the shortest possible time.

The provocation was planned, organized, and carried out with the help of criminals hired in Odessa by the Zionists' unquestionably militant wing, who were the first to smash the windows of Jewish synagogues and apartment buildings, then attacked civilians. Local residents, intoxicated by these provocative articles, joined in this evil example as useful idiots. The alleged motive was the bizarre murder of fourteen-year-old Mikhail Rybalchenko in Dubasari on the eve of Easter. The Chisinau daily newspaper " Bessarabets " published an article about a possible ritual murder, as police allegedly reported that the body was found with its eyes, ears, and mouth sewn shut, with cuts on its veins and rope marks on its hands.

Another article reported that one of the murderers of Jews had already been caught and had revealed the details of the crime. It reported that a baptized, devout teenager had been followed, kidnapped, and drained of blood as a goy, with the intention of using his sacrificial blood in some sacred ritual.

The unusual articles caused a stir and agitated gossip among the city's residents, heightened the imaginations of the townspeople, and aroused pre-existing prejudices and superstitions against Jews... Moreover, rumors had been circulating among the population for two months before Passover.

The police conducted a prompt investigation into the teenager's murder, uncovered all the details of the case, and found the culprit.

It all turned out to be a lie. The teenager's real killer was later identified as his uncle, the cause of a fight over an inheritance. The boy died from multiple stab wounds, not blood loss. No stitches were found on his eyes, ears, or mouth.

The newspaper " Bessarabets " published an official refutation of the previously published false information. The autopsy report on the teenager was also published. But public unrest did not subside. Meanwhile, a rumor spread through the city that the Russian Tsar had allegedly signed a secret decree authorizing the killing and robbing of the descendants of Christ's murderers for three days after Easter. A week before the holiday, unknown individuals scattered leaflets in public places, calling on virtuous Christians to take active action against the Jews, in the name of their father, the Tsar.

Alarmed by the explosive self-hatred, the Jewish community, with a delegation of authoritative figures, appealed to the Provincial Administration for assistance and protection, and simultaneously to the Bishop of Chisinau and Khotyn, asking him to speak out against the blood libel and calm the unrest. The delegations were received and listened to attentively, but the measures taken following the meeting were insufficiently reliable.

Bessarabian Governor V.S. Raben ordered increased police presence and patrols in the city during Easter, especially in Jewish neighborhoods.

But Metropolitan Jacob took no action. Jews later accused him of once expressing his opinion in a private circle: "...it is pointless to deny the fact that the Jewish sect "Khusid" practices drinking Christian blood in secret from their fellow believers."

CHAPTER 3

Every person will taste death. All is decay: name, body, legacy, life's work, property. Only faith in God will endure forever, tested for perseverance. Therefore, life is worth living only by His Law.

Perhaps the best answer to this question comes from a Ukrainian taxi driver named Bogdan. I hired him to help me drive a car from Moscow to Samara. He turned out to be an interesting guy, with experience in racketeering and corruption, and also a candid personality who enjoys discussing his personal life. Here are his observations from this life lesson.

The Jews have muzzled all the world's media. Now, no one anywhere, in any country, even from the world of politics or economics, will dare to oppose the Zionists. Taking advantage of this, these people have begun to infiltrate all major and minor television, radio, and printed media, and are already browsing the internet, where they will soon take over everything. They have become skilled in usury and have introduced their developments into the so-called banking system, and with this now legalized scam, they have legally captured the global Christian world. We Christians, forgetting the prohibitions of our religion, have blindly succumbed to the temptations of the devilish charms of Judaism. The Jews, using the maneuvers of the media and banks, have brought the entire judicial system under their control worldwide. They are deliberately creating a web of red tape in legal proceedings.

"Why do they need this?" "To rule the world. In any court, there will be a winner and a loser. They've masterfully learned to use this. The legal process has become a lever for them to pressure authorities around the world. Believe it or not, it's been like this for a long time. They're everywhere."

So, I worked like a donkey in Kharkiv for five years in the city's public services system, building a team of professionals in three small businesses, uniting them around common interests. We slowly began restoring everything: water mains, sewerage systems, and established 24/7 emergency response teams. The prices were reasonable, the quality excellent. The mayor's office couldn't be happier with us, and we've also made some money. We bought minivans and all sorts of specialized equipment, and leased the territory of a former motor transport company with the option to purchase it later. Everything seemed great, so live and enjoy. Improve, develop, invest in new projects.

But then the Jews came, swarming in from all directions, unexpectedly. The new deputy mayor started conducting audits, the new deputy banker started stalling transactions and payments, and problems started to pile up. The disputes ended up in court out of nowhere; no one owed anyone anything, no one suffered losses, no client complaints, but these devils found something to pick on.

Before these events, two or three years ago, there was a shortage of pipes on the market, and to save time, we bought them from private sellers directly at the market. We formalized the transactions on the spot, in writing. It would say, "Such-and-such a small enterprise bought so-and-so many meters of pipes from such-and-such a person with the last name such-and-such for such-and-such a price." But some of the traders didn't have passports or trade licenses, and this circumstance allegedly became grounds for suspending their businesses two years later. The same thing happened at the bank. Fines were a good thing, of course. But no, they decided to go to court to determine the damages we caused with our carelessness.

The trial dragged on for almost a year and a half. In the first two months of our small businesses' shutdown, we lost our best specialists. It's understandable—everyone has families, wives, children, and obligations. Then we had to pay urgent debts, rent for land and buildings, and pay salaries for office staff. We started investing our savings and selling our specialized equipment. And then, bankruptcy.

So do you know how it all ended? You'll never guess.

So, briefly. Everything that was ours became theirs. Everyone who belonged to the three MPs became the "Mir" association. The owner and also the president is David Abramovich Volk. He's also a friend of the judge, a relative of the prosecutor, the deputy mayor's in-law, and even our lawyer, whose last name is Ivanov, turns out to be in on them. You see, they're all kikes. The bastards ate me up. And believe me, it's the same all over the world.

CHAPTER 4

Retribution for violating God's Law awaits its hour. Punishment comes irreversibly. Angels act always and only in accordance with Divine command, invisibly punishing some people at the hands of others. This just principle of life on earth maintains balance in a world tossed by passions. Throughout the seven veils of heaven and throughout the earthly realm, hosts of angels dwell and are present, sowing grace in the world by the command of Allah the Most High. They do not distinguish between good and evil, and therefore, in this thicket of manifestations of rainbow light and goodness, every God-fearing person can receive generous gifts, while the dishonest, the greedy, and even the peddler of lies can receive an undeserved gift.

Before the creation of man, the Lord of the worlds, Allah, the Exalted and the Most High, created the creations of the ancestors of the future house-elves, the faithful asexual beings Al-Him and Al-Bim, who, during the Age of Evil, were oppressed and persecuted by the misguided, sinful jinn who had embarked on the criminal path of unbelief and who perpetrated atrocities against them. At an urgent time, Allah the Most High created man and recognized him as His best creation, superior to the angels and the stars in the sky. The remaining Al-Him and Al-Bim, the survivors of the Genocide, decided to seek salvation wherever they could, somewhere near the descendants of the forefather Adam.

Allah, the Most High, even creates that which is unknown to us. Many good jinn died in the flow of time during the long, endless extraterrestrial millennia, and afterward, the number of wicked, evil tyrants increased among them. Angels subsequently began to exterminate them everywhere for their crimes and blasphemy. And miraculously, by divine command, only one righteous jinn remained after the execution of the rebels who had transgressed God's law. He glorified the beautiful names of Allah, the Most High. For this, he was granted the unprecedented protection of the Creator of heaven and earth: to dwell among the angels in the Seventh Heaven, to admire the Lotus of the Ultimate Limit, the Sidrat al- Muntaha tree , to hear the singing of angels, and from there to attain longevity. According to legends that do not claim to be reliable, his name was supposedly Azazal , but this is not confirmed anywhere in the Holy Quran or in the prophetic Sunnah.

Life has many roads, paths , routes, pleasant encounters, and a million adventures. And many travel companions. But they say there's no one dearer or sweeter than one, even if you share it with a scoundrel or just anyone... The road home.

Every person must move in the murky haze of an unknown path, constantly hoping that he has taken his next step in the right direction according to the Law of Allah Almighty and that it was the best choice of all possible in fate.

Every nation trudges along in a swaying crowd behind those ahead, jostling each other in an unknown land, hoping that the best among them, with a good sense of space and time, are leading the way. But it's a disaster if the nation lacks a common goal for a successful journey, and if society doesn't have a leader worthy of his qualities and talents at its helm.

Anything poorly assembled and crookedly glued is easily destroyed; a shake or a jolt is enough. Let's start with our forefather Adam: he wasn't Jewish. Neither was the prophet Nuh (Noah) or his son Shem (from whom the Semites supposedly descend). Then there's the prophet Ibrahim (Abraham), and suddenly the unreality sets in: we see and hear that he turns out to be the forefather of the Jewish people, the chief of the three patriarchs. The other two prophets in

Islam, Isaac (Isaac among the Jews and Isaac among Christians) and Jacob (Yacob and Jacob), one being the son, the other the grandson. Peace and blessings be upon all the prophets. There are many questions, but they obscure all the answers with a fog of chatter, all sorts of exotic veils complicated by tiny, intricate ornaments and patterns to obscure clarity of thought. At the end, they'll pose their own questions, including, "What do you think?" And so it goes, everywhere and in everything, they'll argue—their method is window dressing.

But we've spent decades studying the nature of their cunning minds, examining the underlying circumstances, and we understand this enthusiasm for cheap tricks that work for centuries. Why? One of the full answers is that the human lifespan is short. Individuals and society as a whole never have enough time to clean out these Augean stables... We know why they don't recognize the Prophet Ibrahim (Abraham) as the forefather of the Arabs, Assyrians, Lebanese, Palestinians, Maltese, and other peoples. How does this work in their heads?

Khalilullah is a nickname for the Prophet Ibrahim (Abraham), meaning "friend of Allah." The 14th surah of the Quran is named after the Prophet (peace and blessings be upon him). He is the Messenger and preacher of monotheism, the ancestor of the Arabs and Jews; every Muslim, when praying the Salavat prayer, mentions his name and blesses his descendants twice. It was he, along with his son, the Prophet Ismail, who restored the temple in Mecca, destroyed by time, and it was he who installed in the wall the stone brought by the angel Jibril (Gabriel), peace be upon him. But why do the Jews not only not talk about this, but are completely silent about it?

God announced, and the Archangel Gabriel (peace be upon him) conveyed to the Prophet Abraham that he would become the father of many children, the founder of a great nation. And he never doubted this.

Ishmael, the firstborn, was born to the servant Hagar when he was 86 years old, and his second son, Isaac, was born to the elderly Sarah when he was 100 years old. He had a third wife who bore many children.

Here is an episode from the Torah (Old Testament) that tells of the misfortunes of Hagar (the servant of the prophet Abraham's wife Sarah) and her son Ishmael.

The prophet Abraham and Sarah were elderly and childless. Abram's wife, Sarai, bore him no children (Genesis 16:1). Sarai had an Egyptian servant named Hagar. One day, Sarai said to Abram, "Behold, the Lord has restrained me from bearing children. Now go in to my servant; perhaps I shall have children by her." Abram heeded Sarai's words. Then Sarai, Abram's wife, took Hagar her Egyptian servant, after Abram had lived ten years in the land of Canaan, and gave her to Abram her husband as a wife. He went in with Hagar, and she conceived (Genesis 16:2-4). Her son was named Ishmael. A few years later, Sarah also gave birth. Her son was named Isaac. On the day Isaac was weaned, Abraham held a great feast: "And Sarah saw that the son of Hagar the Egyptian, whom she had borne to Abraham, mocking her son, said to Abraham, 'Cast out this slave woman and her son, for the son of this slave woman will not inherit with my son Isaac'" (Genesis 21:9-10). Although Abraham did not like these words, he did as Sarah wished. God promised him that Hagar's son would also become a great nation (Genesis 21:12-13). After this, Abraham, having provided Hagar and Ishmael with bread and water, sent them away, and they set out on a long journey through the desert. In the desert, the lonely wanderers ran out of water, and they both were in danger of dying of thirst. Hagar, leaving Ishmael under a bush, retreated to a bowshot's length, so as not to witness her son's death throes. She sat down on the ground and wept bitterly. Salvation in such circumstances was almost impossible. But! At that moment, an angel appeared to her and said, "God has heard the voice of the lad...arise and take him by the hand, for I will make of him a great nation." (Genesis 21:17-18) The Lord "opened Hagar's eyes," and she saw a well of water. As a result, Hagar and her son were saved.

Let's begin with the assertion that the words of Allah Almighty are the truth, and therefore the statements in the Holy Scriptures must be undoubtedly true and indisputable. Yet here there are so many liberties and inaccuracies.

Here Hagar is a servant, and then suddenly it is indicated during her expulsion that she was already a slave.

Such a colorful story about the romantic birth of Ishmael, when the prophet Abraham was already 86 years old, and suddenly the birth of Isaac, when Sarah was 90 years old, and the prophet Abraham was already 100 years old, is presented simply as a statement of fact without any delightful precursor to the miracle.

And then, supposedly, Ishmael, already 15, mocks his one-year-old younger brother. Everything is immediately obvious and clear; the plot was written and rewritten many times, hence the distortions and a clearly artificially constructed narrative.

The story of the supposed sacrifice of Isaac in the Torah and the Prophet Ishmael in the Quran must also be brought into play here. Why is Isaac presented as an only son in the Torah (Old Testament)? These facts are indisputable and compelling; they demonstrate human involvement in the writing of the Torah's texts.

The noble Quran describes everything clearly and concisely, the hadiths contain clear commentaries, and the Almighty God, the Holy One, is always merciful and compassionate to His creation. The event of the sacrifice of his only son, the 12-year-old compassionate righteous man Ishmael, a son obedient to his father, occurred. For his devotion and faith in the Merciful and Compassionate God, the Almighty Allah replaced the son's sacrifice with a yearling ram. God, through the Archangel Gabriel, rewarded the prophet with the news that his elderly wife Sarah would give birth to a son, Isaac. On this site, on the ruins of the ruined temple of the forefather Adam, the forefather Ibrahim, together with his son Ishmael, would build the Kaaba. Here, as a sign of the necessity of shedding blood, the first human would undergo circumcision . Prophet Ibrahim circumcised his son Ismail.

Read the Divine Quran and you will find nothing superfluous or flawed, no vaguely worded words, no inaccuracies, no errors, and this in itself testifies to its authenticity and the absence of human intervention. Everything in the Quran is good and true, and it cannot be destroyed, distorted, or forgotten, for the Almighty preserves it in the memories of the hearts and souls of millions of living people.

In the book of Genesis (22:11-19), God called Abraham to offer his beloved son Isaac as a burnt offering in the land of Moriah , on one of the mountains. Stunned, Abraham obeyed . On the third day of their journey, Abraham and Isaac arrived at the place God had indicated. Arriving there, Abraham built an altar, bound Isaac, laid him on the altar on the wood, and was about to raise the knife over him when an angel called to him from heaven, "Abraham! Abraham!" He said, "Here I am." The angel replied, "Do not lay your hand on the boy, nor do anything to him, for now I know that you fear God, seeing you have not withheld your son, your only son, from Me." (Gen. 22:11-12)

Everything in the text is absurd and preposterous. The Almighty God knows everything, His words are true and flawless. However, this clearly reveals an artificially constructed narrative. First, the prophet Abraham was 137 years old, his son Isaac was 37.

Secondly, Isaac was not the only son, he could have been the favorite, of course, because his brother Ishmael was alive and at that time he was about 50 years old. In the Bible, the book of Genesis indicates that he lived 137 years.

Judaism originally lacked the concepts of heaven and hell. This theme first appeared in Maimonides' reflections on reincarnation in

Gilgulim . Rambam discussed the afterlife and the concept of heaven and hell in terms drawn from Quranic texts, undoubtedly to clarify these concepts for the Jewish people. Heaven, the highest reward for the righteous who achieve perfection through their qualities, is called Gan Eden—a place of spiritual bliss from closeness to God. Hell, on the other hand, is Gehenna , where sinners undergo a process of purification through pain and temporary suffering.

CHAPTER 5

The brownie shriveled into a ball of terror. And for over a month, he showed no signs of life...

This incomprehensible to these pores Weird disturbing story started in Moscow on parking near restaurant Arbat on old Kalininsky The case continued on the avenue and, by the end of 2007, has still not concluded. At least, I know nothing about the outcome. And all this despite so many interested parties involved in this case, including officials with real power and authority, many others from law enforcement and regulatory agencies who undoubtedly participated in the investigations, people who testified, and, of course, the suffering of the relatives and friends who suffered an irreparable loss .

Ruslan and I Abduvakhapov stood at ours cars under boring absent-minded It was raining, unusual for such a time of year , and we were smoking and discussing the ongoing problems at work when a suspicious-looking stranger ran up to us. He was a tall, agitated man, unkempt and painfully thin, in his late twenties. It was February-March 2006; it's hard to pinpoint the situation, as we were going through all sorts of difficulties in our business at the time, and the months had become so dense that the days flew by...

"Excuse me," he began his speech, stuttering...

"You guys, you seem like serious people, like cool kids... Save my life, for God's sake. I'm being pursued by a cult, a gang of bloodsuckers, and with them are the mafia cops, the killers. They want to kill me too, so I'll keep quiet..."

I just jumped from the second floor in these rags, I couldn't even take my valuables or money, I only grabbed my passport, I was in such a hurry when they broke down the doors. If we don't leave here now, they'll catch me.

- Ruslan, let's help the man, let's take him far away from here,

"I barely had time to suggest it when dark shadows of about a dozen people appeared from behind a nearby house, looking around as they ran, searching for their target. We leisurely got into the car, and just as we were heading toward the exit, we began to hear shots fired at us from afar—clearly not from the police, as one of the bullets hit the back of our Toyota Camry, the sound distinct.

Ruslan, who took part in the war, even he became agitated, his voice, always quiet and reasonable, broke into a shout.

- Rahman, where are we going? Think faster? Those bitches are calling someone...

My thoughts were racing through my head, chaotically analyzing the situation, and without any direction, I suggested we head toward the guest apartment. We headed toward Paveletsky Station, where our company rented an apartment nearby for guests who had previously frequently arrived with business assignments from partners specialized in agribusiness.

But the narrow-minded amateurs who arrived from St. Petersburg and occupied lucrative positions in ministries everywhere produced so many bylaws and regulations that they completely destroyed the thriving Agromarket sector for several years. Agriculture was in turmoil, and it was as if it was being deliberately shaken from above, from the Ministry, Parliament, the Presidential Administration, and, occasionally, from the Heavenly Chancellery...

Now the apartment was empty and at the end of the month we had to return the housing to our employee from whom we rented it... All the way we asked the stranger questions and received confused, abrupt answers that did not give a general picture of the vision of the subject of the case.

CHAPTER 6

And the Lord called unto Moses, and spake unto him out of the tent of meeting, saying,

Speak to the children of Israel and say to them: When any of you brings an offering to the Lord, then you shall bring your offering of the herd and the flock, if it is of livestock. (LEVITICUS Chapter 1.1, 1.2)

This evening will remain etched in everyone's memory, even against their will. We sat in an uncomfortable, smoke-filled apartment and realized that we would never have been able to offer such surreal speech, much less believe the words of this man, so exhausted and almost completely disheartened by the total persecution of some all-powerful criminal organization or mafia clan. But what we ourselves had experienced over the last couple of hours literally forced us to believe his every word without a doubt. The trust was absolute.

In general, I will try to systematize his story in the order I understood it, and not in the confused and confusing way he told us then.

The man's name was Alexey. He'd arrived in Moscow from Krasnoyarsk some time ago, hoping to blend in among the crush of millions. He had a cousin, Dmitry, a successful businessman and vagabond nicknamed "Uzbek," who had quickly built up his fortune. He decided to hole up with him, find some money, and go somewhere permanent, somewhere in Europe. There were many reasons for fleeing Krasnoyarsk. The main one was that he was in the wrong place at the wrong time.

He and a girl named Polina, on a romantic date, witnessed a ritual sacrifice involving the murder of several teenagers. During his stay in the capital, Alexey, for obvious reasons, never spoke to anyone from his hometown by phone, much less his family and friends. For the same reasons, he lived the life of an ascetic hermit to avoid being accidentally exposed. His cousin, Dima, is a naturally silent man; you can't get too much out of him, a man of principles. He didn't ask or pry anything . When they saw each other several years later, all they did was hug and exchange a few bits of information about relatives, acquaintances, and the latest news from the city. That was it.

After which Dimon asked directly:

- Are you having problems? Serious ones or what? Do you need help?

"I didn't want to tell him anything extra, or let him in on this nonsense. I told him we needed to get by here for a while, needed an apartment where we could hide out for a while, so we could quietly, somehow, without the cops noticing, quickly get the paperwork done and go somewhere abroad."

There was no talk of money. It was my savvy brother who rented that abandoned, cool apartment in the very center, and even located on the second floor, so it would be easier to leave if something happened. He thought of everything, even gave me a few thousand bucks to keep me going.

Dmitry is half Uzbek, completely unlike Russians, with a different mentality, even though he never saw his father. When he was born, his boss was already behind bars. His father, Abbas Otkirov , was a criminal figure, a brutal man, a real man of action; I remember him. My brother-in-law was often at our house, coming with his aunt Nastya, the younger sister of my father, Boris Pavlovich Vodopyany . He always helped our family with gifts and money during those turbulent times of change with Perestroika.

Everything was expensive at the market, the stores were empty, there was nothing but dry imported milk and Soviet bread.

He was the one who bought me my first bike for my birthday. He was a big shot, even though he worked as a simple judo coach at the Dynamo sports club. It's a shame he was a smart guy, but he was jailed for extortion and racketeering. Just before his release from prison in the 1990s, some convict who'd suddenly gone crazy with delirium tremens killed him in a dream with a shank. Later, eyewitnesses recounted how the poor rascal, crying and swearing in his cell, swearing that an invisible spirit had been torturing his mind for a long time, forcing him to suffer, and that this had led to the murder. Of course, he got a little thrashing for his lawlessness and some bruising from his family, so he crossed himself and went to his boss to confess his sin, frankly.

So, somehow, Dmitry inherited some of his father's facial and personality traits. A quick-witted little brother beyond his years, even though he's only just over twenty, he can do anything, and he'll go far if he doesn't get into trouble. God forbid!

Based on all this, I don't understand how these cops or anyone else were able to find me in Moscow?

- Alexey asked this rhetorical question to himself and to us.

CHAPTER 7

The lips of the crooked ones with bloody foam are not stupid.

They consider other people to be animals.

Ruslan and I listened to Alexey's revelations with heavy hearts. The chill of the room intensified the experience, as one after another dark images of horrific scenes, a heartbreaking spectacle beyond words, appeared in our minds. Silence fell over the room.

We sat frozen, motionless, absorbing this nightmarish information with every fiber of our being through that uneven, trembling, shifting voice, richly tinged with emotional notes. It somehow penetrated my mind with mystical information and virtual images, filling it with a caustic, pulsating content until my temples ached, and from there it reached my heart, causing me to feel a pain in my chest for the first time in my life. For a split second, my heart felt so tight that I unconsciously placed my right hand on the spot. Ruslan must have felt something similar at that moment, unable to bear the tension, and he muttered,

"It's impossible to tolerate such a draft," he went and closed all the vents in the windows.

After finishing school, Alexey had an unsuccessful start to adult life. He wanted to enroll at Krasnoyarsk State University, but while applying, he accidentally became involved in an unforeseen incident involving a friend of his with Chechens and Ingush. A verbal argument and mutual insults between different ethnic and cultural groups escalated into a fight, which eventually led to a savage, merciless stabbing. Much blood was shed, for no apparent reason.

This always happens when people live without the Almighty God in their hearts, minds, and souls, not understanding His laws. Several Caucasians were seriously stabbed, and the Vainakhs also injured many others. Fortunately, no one was killed, but the authorities brought all those involved in the bloody clash to trial.

Due to his age, and of course the court took into account his first conviction for inflicting particularly grievous injuries with a bladed weapon with a threat to life, Alexey received a seven-year general regime prison sentence for several charges combined, of which he served three years.

He was released on parole. He didn't want to pursue higher education while living off his parents. Instead, he decided to sensibly help his father in his difficult business in any way he could, and not just with his brain.

During a difficult time testing the family's strength, while his son was serving time in a penal colony, his father, in order to distract himself from his mental anguish, decided to fully engage in a serious, responsible task—working face-to-face with numerous strangers, repairing their personal movable property, all of whom were diverse in every way, status, and social standing, and who would also have financial relationships with each other. To this end, he resourcefully purchased a small plot of land on a vacant lot, which local residents had turned into an informal dump, about ten meters from a densely populated area on Svobodny Avenue. With the help of his sister, Nastya, he managed to secure a substantial loan from a commercial bank with low interest rates, and thus opened a small car service station.

There were plenty of customers, as expected, so we worked 24/7, in three shifts. We mainly handled minor chassis repairs, bodywork, painting, and tire service. Over time, we recruited some tough guys, all experienced in their field, and conflicts rarely arose.

From his verbosity with small details and the warmth in his voice, it was definitely clear that Lesha loved his city, was proud of his parents and relatives in general.

CHAPTER 8

For forty years the prophet Moses led his former slaves, enlightening his blasphemous people, lost in sin...

No matter how much his parents begged and demanded, he still couldn't find a decent girl, in his opinion, whom he could confidently marry without fear of being branded a loser the next day, having tied the knot with, God forgive her, a common slut. Alexey smoked frequently, and his hands shook violently the whole time, especially when he started talking about this exotic date.

Routine life is a barren wasteland of disappointment, seemingly devoid of a spiritual connection with God. You live as if for yourself and as if to do something useful for your family and friends, but in the end, everything turns out to be a disaster for everyone: resentments, tears, disagreements, quarrels with curses and foul language. All good intentions are wasted due to the emptiness of meaning, and the end result is always the bankruptcy of ideas. Aimless spending of time is essentially a meaningless existence. Boredom inevitably leads to something bad, let alone dangerous. "So what, then?" As always, the answer is always: drinking, partying, extreme sports, and fornication. Drink, eat, eat, drink, and then go looking for trouble.

I remember that Saturday, after hanging out with friends at a beer bar, I decided to get a haircut. We'd gotten caught up in watching the live broadcasts of the English Premier League, rooting for Chelsea, who were on their way to the championship for the second year in a row. Abramovich, the Jewish owner of the club, had promised our little tsar Putin a gift – another European championship for the Russian world.

So, in high spirits, I went into a salon downtown to see a hairdresser I knew, but he wasn't there. I was about to leave, when a short, blonde chick with substantial bustlines asked me, "Did you want a haircut or a style?" And so the conversation began... Smiles, jokes, anecdotes, and some savory sexual innuendo.

Then we sat with her at a restaurant, really relaxing, dancing, hugging, kissing, and finally craving something sweet. I wanted to book a hotel room, but she suggested a romantic trip to a midnight theater at some factory's Palace of Culture. She said friends might see her at the hotel, or someone else might remember her as a slut, and then goodbye to her reputation. She confessed that I have keys to the front door of the artists' studio; I'd made a duplicate just in case. There's a spot there where you can set up a ladder and climb up the wall to the landing where the costume designer's warehouse is. Then you can climb up the fire escape to the roof. The creative intellectuals have created a cozy nest in the attic: there's a table, dishes, a sofa, even a telescope for admiring the starry sky; from there, the stage is in full view.

Tomorrow is Sunday, their day off, so there shouldn't be anyone there right now. He says, "Get some Marlboro Lights , some good drinks and snacks, some water and drinks, and definitely some wet wipes. Let's go there, you'll love it, especially me with my scorpion on my butt."

So , we bought everything we needed. We took a taxi to some Palace of Culture and entered the building through a secret door on the side of the first floor. I caught my head on a dead branch of a bush while trying to open the lock; I almost lost an eye from being drunk. In the dark, we found a wooden ladder in the hallway and propped it up against the wall where Polina had pointed. We climbed it one after another, first she, then me with the bags, then we climbed the iron ladder to the attic.

It was cozy, warm, even comfortable. Thanks to two small opening windows, it wasn't dark; at least we quickly set the table. We drank, ate, and passionately indulged in sex on the rickety, creaking sofa. Just as we were finishing this sketch, the loud sound of large doors opening near the stage was heard. Several police officers with large stars on their shoulder straps entered, loudly shouting commands to their units over radio transmitters. Then, one by one, they reported the situation around the area to a nondescript, stooped man, imposingly dressed for late April in a long brown sheepskin coat with a huge light collar and a cap, and departed.

A GAZ Gazelle minibus, carrying passengers, entered the building from the left. A large crowd of people, mostly men, emerged from the main entrance and walked down the aisle between the rows of seats to meet them. Everyone was dressed for the occasion. The men wore formal black suits and coats, along with crisp white shirts, dark ties, and bow ties. There were three or four women, also wearing black coats and red dresses. Every single one of them was wearing headgear: those with beards wore black hats, those with long beards wore exotic, high-brimmed dark fur caps, and the young men wore small, round white yarmulkes. The women, standing in the far corner of the auditorium, wore matching black bonnets with veils. All of these people were clearly in good spirits, or trying to maintain their composure for courage, joking about something and encouraging each other with gentle pats.

Finally, several important figures arrived, among them, apparently, a small old man, the most influential. The bastard smiled, was polite to everyone, and managed to say something to everyone, returning their greetings. He called over a man in a cap and gave instructions, who quickly left the room to carry out the order. At that moment, someone in a hat with long strands of hair at his temples, smiling with a smile that revealed his snow-white teeth, extended his hand in greeting and attempted to shake the old man's. The old man jerked his hand away, raised his voice, and began shouting angrily at him in a foreign language that sounded like German.

CHAPTER 9

Tests of willpower and spirit on the battlefield of passion are perhaps what life is all about. It can be difficult in everyday life to suppress the personal ego (nafs), to smooth over flaws and shortcomings, to constantly display high nobility and generosity of spirit, avoiding the doubts of base passions, demonstrating only character traits and talents... All these attributes are inherent only to those who believe in God's Law. Faith in God is peace.

Polina and I felt like we hadn't even been breathing the entire time. We sobered up instantly, overcome by the sheer curiosity of the experience. Like partisans, we wiped ourselves with wet wipes, quickly dressed, and began to watch like thieves, managing, incidentally, to kiss and hug. This beast got fired up and proposed a second act in front of such a crowd. I wasn't opposed, but something vaguely bothered me. It was the reason I couldn't get the urge to. Tension hung in the air; I could feel the turbulence in the air of this soulless Palace of Culture on my skin; it smelled like evil.

Young men in white skullcaps led seven teenagers out of the Gazelle, two of whom were particularly tall and large, dressed identically in long, bright yellowish-brown coats without hats. Men approached them in a chaotic manner, first older, then younger, seemingly giving each child money. They stroked them, patted their cheeks, hugged them tenderly, and one kissed each one on the head with compassion and kindness. Women approached to relax the children, giving them candies and sweets and uttering a litany of endearing words. One plump woman with large, outlandish gold bracelets on her wrists and numerous beautiful, sparkling ornaments on her neck, ears, and fingers brought with her a heavy box of Coca-Cola cans. She opened the box and handed each child a can.

From somewhere behind the stage, the young people dragged a long dining table and were honored by everyone gathered. Men in fur hats unloaded boxes and sacks from a Gazelle van.

Suddenly the gates opened and another Gazelle, a truck with sides, drove in, an unusually large wooden barrel was rolled out of it, after which everyone clapped their hands, someone tried to sing songs solemnly like psalms, but no one supported him, and he fell silent.

At this point, the old man lit a fire in a wooden barrel using a multitude of crumpled paper balls. When the fire flared brightly, he began tossing some bundles of compressed herbs into it; the fire burst into flames and crackled with sparks. The little man, holding his long curls at his temples and his beard with one hand, covered the barrel with an iron lid with the other. A moment later, he lifted it and set it aside, clouds of fragrant smoke filling the large space.

Everyone slowly began to leave the auditorium, heading outside. Smoke began to rise, and I suggested Polina go outside, too, but the naughty girl, kissing my ear, began playfully and restlessly fingering my penis. When it hardened, she began sucking it very slowly, with a tactile tenderness that thrilled my bloodstream to the point of dizziness, and with feigned pleasure.

It is worth making a remark here, Ruslan interrupted Alexey's lustful memories with a sharp attack,

- It's you. Let's not get distracted by the dirty details. Unnecessary ones.

"I added a drop of a different opinion," I said,

"Tell it like it is, without lies. Ruslan doesn't like it when people lie, and neither do I. But we need all the details now so we know what to do and who to involve in investigating this terrible case. You said they killed the children and they want to finish you off."

- Having said obediently:

- Got it, bros. I'll be more specific from now on.

Alexey stood up and went to the bathroom to relieve himself, while Ruslan and I got into an argument. We disagreed on Lesha's future. Ruslan and I hadn't been getting along for some time, though we'd been like brothers for seven or eight years. My arguments, as often happened, proved more compelling; I convinced him more with eloquence than logic, although it's hard to say. Often, in life, it's simply the instinct for self-preservation that rules.

Then we decided to take a walk and buy some essentials and groceries for a snack. We went out into the courtyard and carefully examined the car. We spent a long time shining our phone flashlights on the bodywork, but found no bullet marks; the bullet must have ricocheted off the underside of the car. We went to the grocery store around the corner. We bought cigarettes, flatbreads, samsa, cheese, a bar of Kazakhstan chocolate, halal shawarma, salads, various drinks, and plenty of single-serving coffee and tea bags . Most importantly, we didn't forget to stock up on wet wipes, toothpaste, and toothbrushes.

When we returned to the apartment, Ruslan quickly began rolling a joint into a long Belomorkanal cigarette. I, taking a large towel from the stack of new ones in the closet, went to take a shower.

When he returned, the table in the dining room was already set. Soon, the kettle in the kitchen began to whistle, boiling. Everyone brewed their own tea or coffee. Everyone was silent, slowly chewing their almost-cold shawarma with distracted jaws. Ruslan broke the silence with a question,

"Brother, this joint isn't giving me the thrill, maybe we should have some whiskey? May Allah the Almighty forgive us sinners, it's not every day that things like this happen. They shoot at us, we run, with nothing in our pockets to fight back. If only I had my Stechkin with me, I'd show those bastards how to fight in a city. You know what I mean?"

"I thought silently. Taking advantage of the pause, Ruslan took a liter of Black Label whiskey from the bar and generously poured it into glasses almost to the brim. They all drank without clinking glasses, as is customary at funerals for Orthodox Russians. It seemed to ease off a bit immediately; at least it became easier to breathe. They lit up. And then Alexey said into the silence, mysteriously casuistically, his voice breaking into falsetto,

- You won't be able to imagine this. Never. These are beasts. Predators. Executioners.

At that moment, Ruslan suddenly stood up and swung at Alexey. I managed to get between them. He again suggested that we not interfere in the life of a stranger, especially since we had already helped more than we could, risking our lives. I, in turn, countered by saying that we needed to take this information higher up the government hierarchy, perhaps even to the Federation or the Head of the Presidential Administration. They would certainly handle everything according to the law, so that such an ungodly act of cannibalism would never happen again.

Alexei's terrifying words about the children's murders hung in the air of that room, of course, like ghosts, but we couldn't even imagine the details of that horrific event back then. Dark memories, wrought by the alcohol he'd consumed, poured from his lips and rolled like legumes: beans, peas, soybeans, peanuts, but most of all lentils, all a jumble of different colors and flavors, generously topped with tomato. And that bloody vinaigrette is now impossible to forget.

CHAPTER 10

Gather in a circle, necromancers. Let him enter

The Lord Master will come to the center with the grimoire and remove the amulet from the neck.

When smoke The fog cleared and the air noticeably cleared. Workers in blue uniforms and orange hard hats entered the hall from the street, swearing loudly and expertly in Russian. They pushed two powerful heaters with long sleeves of corrugated white pipes closer to the center, almost next to the raised stage, which they then laid out to the sides and turned on. One of them tried to find out what event or celebration the people were attending, but no one bothered to answer his questions. Shrugging his shoulders in bewilderment, the worker nodded, leading his comrades toward the exit.

Intelligent, distinguished-looking men, seemingly from high society, paying no attention to the workers, chose wines to their taste from boxes of different colors and, divided into groups, drank from pot-bellied glasses off to the side, sitting in the spectator seats.

As soon as the last worker left the room, a flurry of activity erupted everywhere. The chief usher apparently ordered everyone to hurry. Voices in different languages could be heard everywhere, all buzzing in incongruous tones like wasps; it was clear they had flown from different nests.

At this moment, a large, oval-shaped, tall cake, decorated with red roses, was placed on the table. At the elder's command, the women quickly began to pay specific attention to the shy boys, smiling as they handed each a piece of cake, always accompanied by a rose on a plate and a teaspoon.

The teenagers, embarrassed but listening to the persuasion of the adults, obediently ate their portions, washing them down with Coca-Cola from cans.

Young men in white skullcaps and light blue gloves scurried around, hurrying quickly. A glossy, varnished, lint-free yellow floor covering with a patterned pattern was laid across the entire stage. They brought four sacks of flour, two large round sieves, a bucket of kitchen utensils, two boxes of various-sized nails, and numerous old hammers of all kinds, no doubt well-used. Almost at a run, they evenly spaced tall, delicate candelabra and large candlesticks with heavy legs across the stage, and piled a pile of white waffle towels at the edge of the linoleum.

A man in black and white gloves handed them several paper boxes containing candles from the audience. The young men quickly began placing the candles in the candlesticks and candelabra.

At this time, one after another, the boys began to feel ill, their heads could not stay on their shoulders, their legs buckled, and their arms began to lose their motor skills, so that everyone's banknotes fell out and scattered across the floor, now fluttering in the warm air currents.

One fat elderly man in a hat and a black suit, from under which many long white threads hung around the entire circumference of his belt, muttering an incomprehensible word like " Tzedakah ," began to clumsily collect the money and put it in his trouser pocket.

The young men lined the children up in a single, long row on the stage. Two thin men, wearing clear medical gloves, optical glasses, and sparse beards, began examining them carefully with bright flashlights and magnifying glasses. First, they quickly and nimbly stripped them naked. They checked their legs, arms, limbs, and skin, especially their heads. They carefully examined their eyes, noses, ears, and pelvises.

Pointing to their penises, they reported something to the elder, who was changing into a ritual robe-like garment, azure in color with dense gold stripes and numerous small buttons. The old man gave a curt command to the fat man with dangling white threads at his belt. The big man, unable to climb from his seat onto the stage, ran and climbed the stairs.

Approaching the defenseless, paralyzed boys, he once again asked the experts to identify any flaws, defects, or imperfections. They did. Kneeling down, he violently twisted the children's heads off, then asked for two empty sacks, into which he stuffed the still-soft, lifeless bodies.

Having completed the murder, he, slowly raising his arms, began to dance around the large, glossy linoleum floor, singing a cheerful tune. Behind him, clapping their hands, other dancers in caps, hats, and skullcaps began to dance, their numbers growing. When the elder joined them, they, all clearly out of their minds, were in a kind of hypnotic trance of intoxication , as if their bodies and senses were in a state of exaltation, their souls in ecstasy.

The mass euphoria added to the excitement, apparently heightening the level when their leader pulled an unusually long match from a giant box. He held it up and showed everyone. The entire merry crowd began chattering and clicking their voices in dissonance. Someone burst into hysterical laughter and screamed, "Adonai!"

Apparently, the room had warmed up, because everyone, including the joyfully laughing women, began to take off their outer garments. The old man struck a match and lit a single thick candle on a golden floor lamp. Then he gave a command, and the entire crowd transformed and, holding hands, continued dancing in a single circle.

The elder walked across the stage, using this candle to light unusual, multi-branched candelabra arranged in alternating rows, each at the same height in the top row and the bottom row. Someone turned off the electric lights, and the room was enveloped in a solemn scene of a demonic sabbath.

Down there, a young guy in a white skullcap and socks began to draw a large pentagram on the linoleum with pink chalk, and on top of it, he placed a Star of David with white chalk.

The old man nodded and waved his hand, giving a signal to the fat man, who shouted:

In some incomprehensible language of gibberish, standing in place, rocking back and forth with eyes closed, wailing, " boo boo boo..."

- They built temples for Baal in the Valley of the Son of Hinnom , to make their sons and daughters pass through the fire in honor of Molech, which I did not command them, and it did not come into My mind that they should do this abomination, causing Judah to sin. (Book of the Prophet Jeremiah, chapter 32, verse 35).

Polina whispered in my ear in a drawn-out voice:

"For some reason, all the candelabras and candlesticks have seven candlesticks." Then, with genuine fear in her voice. "What are we going to do? Lesha, I really need to go to the bathroom, my stomach is already growling."

- I immediately cut her off with a gesture, raising my index finger to my lips. I said briefly:

- Shut up. Be patient. They'll kill us if they find us.

At this time, two people in gloves and glasses began to wipe and smear the defenseless bodies of the children, intoxicated with the potion, with large snow-white rags, dipping the gauze from time to time in some liquid.

When they finished the procedure, the fat man pushed a large wooden barrel forward. The boys carefully lowered the bodies of five teenagers into it, one at a time, chanting mysterious prayer formulas through their teeth. Dipping a brush in red wine, he painted various symbolic crosses from various churches on the backs of three of them; for two, he drew invisible crescent moons with a brush. He then closed the barrel lid tightly behind them and began hammering on it with a mallet to press it more firmly against the arch.

At this point, all the men picked up hammers and nails, began singing incomprehensible songs resembling psalms, and began to line up in an impromptu circle facing each other. The barrel was placed on its side. The leader approached it first, chanted "Elohim Adonai," and hammered a nail into the barrel. The elder then rolled it toward a man standing opposite him, wearing long braided hair at his temples, a tall fur hat, short pants revealing white knee-high socks, and a snow-white cape with blue patterns slung over his shoulder. He quietly muttered something, also hammered a nail, and rolled the barrel toward a man in a hat and glasses, who was shaking a hammer, awaiting his turn. He, with a loud cry, "Yahweh Melech," exhaled, and drove in a large nail with a single blow.

Everyone around them, excited, seemed to be in some mystical state of vulgar, primal ecstasy, clapping their hands frantically, stamping their feet, and reciting prayerful formulas. The procession continued without stopping, some leaving the circle, their places taken by new participants. The last to be driven in were the women, who hammered in small symbolic nails with firm, confident blows.

The barrel was tied with ropes on both ends and attached to the hook of the hoist, lowered from above. A smiling young man in a white skullcap operated the control panel. After confirming the secure connection, the elder allowed the barrel to be hung on the hook. Silently lifting it to just above knee height, the youth rushed to the aid of the nimble old man, who was already heading toward a large stainless steel container. They placed a large stainless steel vat beneath the hanging wooden barrel, and the wrinkled old man clucked his tongue frequently with pleasure.

CHAPTER 11

Baal Zebub is a certain Flying Lord or Beelzebub, the dark ruler of flies, the supreme demon, who loves burnt children's bones.

Molech was the god of fire, to whom animals and children were sacrificed.

Then one of the crazy fanatics, supposedly chosen by God, decided that Yahweh liked the sweet smell of burning children's flesh ...

By this time we had already finished the second bottle of whiskey, and what's interesting is that we were as sober as a judge, so absorbed were we in Alexey's story .

The old man began to pull the wooden chop out of the barrel with large tongs. When he finally succeeded in extracting the pod from its nest, he sniffed it with undisguised pleasure, examined it, and finally, after thoroughly licking it, carefully wrapped it in a handkerchief and tucked it into the side pocket of his jacket. Then he called his young assistant over, and together they turned the barrel as best they could, began to drain the bloody liquid into a large steel container.

At this time, the women, having long since changed their clothes, spread out a thick, large, round-shaped thing on the linoleum, something resembling a tablecloth, and sifted white flour through a sieve onto it, which they took out from sacks lying nearby.

The men, divided into groups, drank red wines of various varieties, quickly twisting corks with corkscrews and opening dozens of bottles. They poured small portions into their glasses, which they immediately set aside. Soon, a whole army of bottles lined up in a row.

When the blood no longer flowed from the barrel but dripped, the master of ceremonies gave the command to a fat man with white threads on his belt. He quickly approached with two white enamel ladles. The elder, carefully and deliberately, cupped his hands together, began scooping up blood from the vat and transferring it to the ladles. When they were full, the fat man brought the ladles to the men waiting with uncorked bottles. They scooped up blood with teaspoons and poured it into the bottles, then screwed the corks back on.

It was disgusting and repulsive to watch how they licked the spoons, how they dipped them with crooked fingers and scraped them off the sides of the ladles, taking out the remains of blood and licking them off.

Two women, taking the same ladles from the men, began scooping up sifted flour and pouring it into a metal vat. The woman with gold jewelry gave commands, while the others followed her instructions precisely. She instructed one to knead the dough with a wooden shovel, another to add the sifted flour, and a third to continue working the sieve.

Soon, all the work was completed. The old man took out his handkerchief, pulled out a chop , and hammered it back in with a wooden mallet. The men in hats, from young men to old men, began collecting their bottles in paper boxes. The women cut the pink dough into many pieces, rolled them carefully in flour, wrapped them in white cloth with blue patterns, and placed them in various bags with inscriptions.

Men in hats loaded a barrel into a truck, and they also lifted the body bags containing the murdered teenagers. Young men in white skullcaps moved quickly around the room, scrubbing and washing the linoleum, assembling candelabras and candlesticks, and rolling up linoleum. All tools, equipment, and kitchen utensils were thoroughly cleaned and rinsed.

Having turned on the electricity, the young men in yarmulkes, armed with flashlights, began to carefully examine everything on the stage and in the room. The fat man followed them, doing the same again, and finally, raising his thumb, indicated the state of the room to the elder. The old man moved toward the exit, clasping his hands behind his back, followed by the other men, women, and youths.

A man in a sheepskin coat and cap entered the building, inspected the premises, whistled into the empty auditorium, turned off the electric lights, and locked the gates from the outside.

CHAPTER 12

A free, democratic Western society... How can we understand and evaluate this? And is it even true? If so, then why is it free? It's as if no one sees how many problems and troubles there are here.

The problem of freedom from morality and ethical guidelines is when all prohibitions are thrown out the window. That is, now everything is allowed—what was previously forbidden.

People call themselves Christians, yet they don't understand God and His Power, they don't observe the Laws of God found in the Holy Scriptures, and they don't practice anything like the way the one they call Jesus Christ lived, spoke, acted, or prayed. He never called himself God, never said, "Worship me." He ate food, drank water, and relieved himself like all ordinary people. He called for the observance and fulfillment of God's Law.

It's incomprehensible that the entire population of European countries—as if hypnotized by priests (with centuries of accumulated delusions and the inherent distortions of consciousness) and receiving their ideas about the world and things through obedient media, film, radio, and books, along with the immoral amendments to the Christian worldview through the faulty arguments of atheists like the "triangular square"—have reached a point where they can safely be called sleepy supporters of a contradictory idea. How was this possible? People who call themselves Christians, deifying Jesus as a god, yet don't live like him and do what he called them to do? He was circumcised, didn't eat pork, prayed as only Muslims pray today, and cursed usury, fornication, gambling, and the lust for profit...

Due to the Zionists and Freemasons' interference in their intellectual and spiritual space through a contrived, cunning technique—a tool for influencing human thinking, pompously called "Psychoanalysis"—modern Americans and Europeans have gone against God's Laws. Ostensibly, this is based on the meaning of liberal values and the obligatory requirement of adhering to the principles of democracy, yet the contradiction between these values is clearly evident.

On the one hand, the insanely vile sins of Sodom and Gomorrah have been abolished, and same-sex marriages are now openly performed, and murder and euthanasia have been permitted. It all began earlier when the impostor Apostle, in the person of the tax collector Saul (Paul), took the liberty of repealing what Yeshua (Jesus) forbade, permitting the consumption of pork. From that moment on, contradictions began to arise between the Law in the Torah and the Gospel, usury was permitted in the sphere of public morality, and circumcision was abolished. Gradually, moral norms lost the clear boundaries permitted by morality and conscience, as if waters had overflowed their banks and flooded beautiful flowering meadows, turning everything into a swamp teeming with the spores of all sorts of dangerous viruses. Now, the blasphemy of usury, with exorbitant interest rates, is officially permitted: for banks, financial institutions, and pawnshops. Now, opposite-sex couples are allowed to live together without a wedding and have children. The crowning absurdity of this series of contradictions is a new taboo.

On the other hand, it's incomprehensible that they've banned human cloning by law. It's their "ace in the hole." Well, this is to preserve the sacred, unshakable dogma that God created man in his own image and likeness. And this is some kind of obscurantist silliness, like liberal democracy?!

Having abolished clericalism, Europeans, Americans, and the elites were taught to listen and think about everything. They, however, stopped dreaming of the eternal and forgot how to think. But as soon as Christians awaken from their hypnosis, come to their senses, and begin to put shameful Zionism in its place, rest assured, their trump card will fall. Humans will be cloned. The dogma that God created man in his own image and likeness will end the existence of priests and the church. The Zionists are awaiting the signal for the hour X.

It turns out that democracy and liberalism are going against the Laws of God.

The same applies to cultural demands, which vary across world religions. Don't these idiots understand that any culture is, first and foremost, a concept, limited by boundaries—taboos and prohibitions. This value has been preserved only in Islam.

- What cannot be proven is

difficult to refute.

We brought in several high-ranking businessmen we knew to help with this case, which resembled a ritual murder involving cannibalism. Through them, we approached Boris Nemtsov, Viktor Ilyukhin, and Gennady Zyuganov through people who "kept the corridors from office to chancery." Ilyukhin called and even met with Hero of Russia Alexander Chekalin of the Russian Ministry of Internal Affairs. Ultimately, it was all a waste of time and money. Everyone demanded proof: the names of the victims, bodies or death certificates, crime scene photographs and videos, etc. No one was interested in a living witness, the crime scene, dates, etc.

Five or six days after we took Alex under our wing, we had to part ways. He was a completely different person, pleasant-looking, calm, reasonable, and laconic. We dressed him up, gave him a crew cut, and he was transformed beyond recognition. During our week of daily communication, we had grown spiritually closer, as evidenced by the fact that Sir Abduvakhapov, instead of shaking hands, gave Alexey a warm hug when we parted. We said goodbye like kunaks (a term used in the Caucasus and Central Asia for people not related to us but who are treasured) who had become close after a group brawl. We provided him with some money to get by and walked him to the front door of the apartment. A cousin nicknamed Uzbek was supposed to be waiting for him downstairs.

At this point, I need to take a break and move far away from the story of Alexei, this unfortunate man. His story is mind-numbing.

Trouble came from an unexpected place...

Lightning flashed like a sword strike.

To awaken consciousness and tune the mind to the vigilance of impartial reasoning... First, it is necessary to reconstruct the accurate chronicle of events and the epochal spirit of the multifaceted protest mood of the time. This was especially true in Christian Europe, then and now, when some ignorant fanatics were seething with fountains of emotion and currents of national energy.

Let's return to the issues of two centuries ago, taking into account the unformed state of a definitive, universal Christian understanding of the Almighty God. If we look at what exists in public opinion and the average person who considers themselves Christian, their illogical understanding of God in the abstract is a sinful blasphemy, elevating the status of man to the level of a God-man, and immediately lowering the significance of God. This is blatant, obvious blasphemy.

For example, one can often hear absurd admirations, which essentially betray the ignorance of people: divine face, divine voice, beautiful as a god, etc... But, no one has ever seen the Supreme God among people.

Let's now consider at least the most primitive human associations and logical combinations of ideas about God. What immediately comes to mind? God is unequivocally Eternal; He cannot die. He is Almighty. He does not eat and, therefore, does not drink. Therefore, He does not relieve Himself. He has no parents, family, wife, or children. As the Creator, He cannot have rivals. He is the Truth and the Absolute. He created everything and everyone in space and time.

He is the sole ruler of all that exists and all created beings within this space and time. He gives, and He takes away. All good comes from the Creator, and all evil comes from the Creator. The creatures created by Him cannot and are not capable of influencing the Creator in any way; they can only address Him unilaterally with requests for mercy and compassion in their addressed prayers with prayer formulas to Him, the Lord of the worlds , including Iblis, who is trying to lead people down the path of sin.

As it is stated in the Quran in Surah Al-Baqarah (The Cow), verse 117, He is the Creator of the heavens and the earth. When He makes a decision, He merely says, "Be," and it comes to pass.

With the existing fog of ideas in the minds of biased billions of people unable to independently navigate the diverse, dubiously interpreted versions of the Gospels, with their mass of blunders and distortions, the creativity of dozens of copyists who contributed to the books of the Bible, with changes and contradictions in the interpretation of depicted scenes, with an incomprehensible cult of the Trinity, and, of course, attacks from ghostly mirages about the absurdities of atheist rebels with utopias about a better social order, the late 18th and early 19th centuries accumulated a mass of critical energy with doubts, and it was necessary to let off steam.

After all, if we look honestly and fairly at the strictness of observing God's Law, then it will certainly turn out and be the case that Christian moral and ethical requirements are fulfilled exclusively as believing parishioners now in the 21st century only and precisely by those who are called Muslims , who observe Islam.

It has now become clear that there are no true Christians left. Church leaders, due to sex scandals within their strict clerical circles involving pedophilia and homosexuality, have lost the trust and respect of a blasphemous, biased society, and are despised even in previously devout Italy and Spain, not to mention other regions. Let's note that these facts were deliberately presented and publicized in the global media, seemingly in the form of centuries-old sacrilege. And again, let's note the fact in whose hands they are... "Who is the enemy of Christianity?!"

So, it turns out that only Muslims remain Christians today. Only Muslim women, like the Holy Virgin Mary, preserve their chastity by wearing hijabs and concealing their beauty from the gaze of strangers . Like Yeshua of Nazareth, known in Islam as the Prophet Isa, only Muslims recite prayers, called namaz, five times a day . Matthew 26:39 says, "And he went a little further and fell on his face, praying, 'O My Father, if it be possible, let this cup pass from me: nevertheless not as I will, but as You will.'"

And this fear of God with devoted submission to the Almighty God, instead of approval and admiration, causes hostility and even condemnation among people who call themselves Christians with a distorted consciousness of God, who themselves, without suspecting it, are in the shadow of the machinations of the Zionist globalists.

- So what was the world like two centuries ago - the 19th century AD?

- What phenomena could characterize it?

Encyclopedists will immediately make generalizations: protectionism, urbanization, colonialism, industrialization, and, of course, the age of wars.

Military men have always played a huge, if not the leading, role in the writing of history in Europe. The evolution of official leaders—chieftain, chieftain, commander, general, tsar, emperor, president—and unofficial ones—shaman, priest, priest, bishop, patriarch, pope. Whatever one might say about this army, they all forced all their ignorant subordinates to obey their commands, forgetting the commandment: Thou shalt not kill.

We probably already figured out about the rulers who, unfortunately, were mostly crazy dictators and essentially tyrants, with rare exceptions to the rule, in history lessons at school.

We already discussed the phenomenon of people, like brownies, loving to gather in large communities at the beginning of the book. This circumstance contributed to the rapid growth and development of cities. Villagers and rural residents sought interesting experiences and new challenges in their material and spiritual lives. Urbanization as a process is, above all, the usually naive dream of the average person to taste freedom, quickly improve their financial situation, and achieve some measure of success with the many opportunities available in the city-states. And, hidden in the subconscious, there's a deeply ingrained religious feeling—the desire to somehow help family and friends, and the ethnic group.

Urbanization, in fact, is the primary reason for the emergence of industrialization. During the transitional phase of several periods of urban life, active minds sought new opportunities, either to exploit society or to create mechanisms for the production of necessary goods and their sale on the market, initially for their own survival, then out of a thirst for enrichment, naturally initially through artisanal means.

Over time, this led to a process of increasing complexity in technical equipment and the emergence of more complex designs for the creation of machines in order to transport fewer goods from the provinces to the city, especially when city dwellers developed tastes, demands, and requirements.

The transition from an agrarian to an urban society led to the development of industrialization, the creation of technical innovation and large-scale industry, and an increase in its share of the economy due to machine production. New forms of labor organization emerged. Initially, there were weavers, shoemakers, tailors, bakers, blacksmiths, and itinerant peddlers of essential goods. Later, all of this began to be organized in a more civilized manner: workshops, cooperatives, forges, workshops, bakeries, and stores.

The application of scientific and technological advances in industrial production has elevated the importance of the state in the monarchical system of government to a new level.

Ideas about other options for political systems for more perfect governance of societies also began to develop in creative minds.

All these elements and competition in the market for goods and services led, over the years, to the emergence of states with a structured tax system, a regular army, stock exchanges, cities with elites and local populations, city government with courts, police, prisons, banks, factories, plants, restaurants, beauty salons, small manufacturing enterprises: furniture, kitchen utensils, dishes, watches, jewelry and stationery, and, of course, suburbs where agricultural products were produced.

Naturally, not all European states developed equally, just as not all city-states could eventually develop into megacities. Here, the concepts of geopolitics and geoeconomics became significant. Moreover, the legacy of Islamic culture and the subsequent epochal events left a deep imprint on the minds and souls of culturally diverse European peoples. The Holy Inquisition, the Reconquista, the Renaissance, Machiavelli's philosophy, and the witch hunts led to the emergence of a new political form of opposition to Christian neighbors in foreign trade. Protectionism.

The monarchical dynasties and aristocracies of Old Europe demonstrated resourcefulness and will to ostensibly protect the interests of local entrepreneurs by providing them with patronage in foreign trade. This meant attempts to restrict the import of goods similarly produced in their own countries, while at the same time ostensibly supporting the production of domestic producers with various tax breaks and levies. The goals were clear and obvious:

increasing national income, employing more people, and thereby raising the people's standard of living.

But the interference of rulers - in the laws of market relations and free trade, in the natural scientific process of exchanging knowledge and achievements, in the sphere of new trends in the areas of providing services to improve the quality of life in elite circles, which gives a message for raising the cultural status of social outsiders - in all kingdoms led to a deterioration in the lives of subjects, a decrease in the economic well-being of peoples, stagnation and a slowdown in the pace of development of societies.

All of the above. Also, the transformation of Jewish moneylenders into seemingly pious bankers, the most successful of whom were able to acquire prestigious lands, estates, and castles, and, as part of the deal, European noble titles: marquis, count, viscount, baron, and knight.

In the face of change, forced to compete with the nouveau riche bourgeoisie and the newly minted nobility of parasitic usurers in the name of regaining success and prosperity, the ancient aristocratic families, pampered by a trouble-free existence, their strength exhausted and their teeth dulled, were losing their influence in the passing era. They needed time to pause and analyze the new challenges of the time, rebuild themselves, and take advantageous positions within the elite, creating zones of influence and distance from the greedy tactics and encroachments of rogues, while also safeguarding their personal security. The impossibility of maintaining enormous palaces, lands, and servants forced some prudent aristocratic dynasties to shed their burdens and sell their ancestral estates. Much real estate was sold at reduced prices, and some deals looked nothing less than outright robbery.

The moneylenders were furious and cut to the quick, sensing their own strength and capabilities, far worse and more cunning than the Merchant of Venice. One moneylender, driven mad by the resulting permissiveness, began negotiations through King George III's younger brother, Duke Edward, about the possibility of purchasing a small royal estate at a very high price and, as part of the deal, acquiring the title of Duke. Strangely enough, no profitable deal materialized. The King's temporary insanity, caused by the influence of the famous brownie Elborz , and, strangely enough, the severe blow dealt to the system of absolute monarchy by the proclamation of the First French Republic, prevented such a precedent from occurring. This event was considered a clear challenge to insolence throughout the empires, leading to numerous difficulties in acquiring noble titles. Soon, several particularly cunning, illiterate and uncultured bankers had their obviously predatory transactions challenged in court and subsequently annulled, after which their titles were declared false...

Yet the power of money had already transcended the whims of monarchs. The most enterprising nobles, taking advantage of their kinship or close relationships with the monarchs, were also able to enrich themselves beyond measure. Seizing the opportunity, they sold small plots of land, gardens with crumbling infrastructure, and unattractive, squalid stud farms with noble titles included in the trade deals at exorbitant prices to former moneylenders seeking to gain entry into Europe's elite by any means necessary. Money flowed from coffers into mended pockets.

All these processes unsettled the minds and hearts of millions of Europeans; many couldn't bear the strain and fell morally, losing all sense of shame. The effects of the blasphemous jinn's attacks were felt across the European continent in the enormous increase in the number of socially marginalized individuals and lumpen proletariat, seemingly out of nowhere. Everything became a tangled mess.

Adventurers provided food for thought, sparking new trends in philosophy and the visual arts, creating masterpieces in poetry and literature, and discoveries in science. High society was consumed by an all-consuming frenzy of passion and permissiveness, and monarchs were bewildered by the mass bacchanalia: public disgrace in many families of the highest aristocracy, with intrigues involving murder by poison, adultery, betrayal, mortgages to usurers, duels, suicides, and so on.

The bourgeoisie, merchants, commodity producers and industrialists, the urban middle class, and influential families managing agriculture, all faced even more difficult challenges. All these troubles arose from the plundering of the people by usurers, which, above all, led to a sharp decline in the level of education among urban populations, particularly in the loss of Christian morality and ethics across all strata of society. The jinn, at Satan's instigation, ruled the masses with immense cruelty; murders, robberies, thefts, and violence increased. Families were ruined, and marriages dissolved before they could even begin. Somewhere, wine and other alcoholic drinks flowed like rivers, people ate opium and coca leaves, smoked cigars and hashish, choked on cakes, roasted cows and pigs on spits, and famous chefs prepared food according to the recipes of the peoples of the Maghreb.

At the same time, individuals at the top and en masse at the bottom of the social ladder of the public masses were perishing or dying a natural death from the mind-burning shame and disgrace of family tragedies, hunger and disease, while true believers, the best people who believed in God, with pure hearts and souls, preserved within themselves the sacred truths...

The most cruel and evil, the cunning and unscrupulous, the insolent and greedy, those willing to kill and use violence, survived. Like a rich, ideological dough, the Lombards added mold to the Christian body instead of yeast; they reduced the cement content of the mortar holding the building's frame by a factor of several times, adding more clay.

As a result, the Colossus with Feet of Clay still looks pretty good on the outside, except for the terrifying gaping cracks visible to the naked eye. But the Jews spit on this idol of passion every day and plaster over the holes with this glue.

All this chaos in the cities and villages needed to be put in order; the Kingdoms were not yet ready for a major war for spheres of influence among themselves.

Therefore, the brains of adventurers, newly minted ugly nobles, decorated with ornaments of coats of arms with ancient aristocratic families, preferring the good life in idleness, with big mouths and fat wallets, lazy, large-headed, bow-legged youths of small stature, but with a legacy of cunning from their fathers, incapable of dancing due to physical characteristics, but compensating for the shortcomings and flaws with the intricacies of a perverted, cunning mind, loving to speculate on all sorts of philosophical topics about witchcraft, about the joys of debauchery in orgies, love and the chosen people, about the feeling of patriotism, about ways to circumvent the law, how to get money from dirt. These gentlemen of fortune spread wonderful tales at balls in palaces everywhere about tempting promising projects in Asian and African countries, abundant with easily accessible riches, and, moreover, populated by savages devoid of any concept of Jesus Christ and the salvation of the soul.

The great geographical discoveries—the expeditions of the Spanish-born Christopher Columbus in 1492, who discovered America, and the Portuguese navigator Vasco da Gama in 1498, who established a route to India—were essentially the precursors to an unprecedented centuries-long genocide of indigenous peoples. The emergence of colonialism undoubtedly began with the emergence of an obscurantist, blasphemous concept of race, which became the prerequisite for future conquests.

Initially, the Spanish and English, under various slogans, began to conquer and exterminate the peaceful populations of the New World in North and South America. The French also joined the race to discover and claim foreign lands in the Americas. A little later, the cunning Dutch captured some territory, but, realistically assessing their strength, they went further and discovered Australia and New Zealand.

But in the late 18th and early 19th centuries, an idealistic view of dividing people into races emerged, along with the extremely extremist ideological belief of racism. This doctrine is based on the idea that humanity consists of three distinct groups, called races, with distinct mental and physical characteristics. These groups are further subdivided into ethnic communities, some of which are superior to others in innate qualities and spiritual distinctions.

Several decades before the discriminatory concept of racism emerged, various schools of anthropologists proposed their own racial classifications, identifying up to seven major races, dozens of minor races, and anthropological types of mixed-race people. In Germany, the concept of dividing humanity into three races—Caucasoid, Mongoloid, and Negroid—was introduced and developed into racist ideology. In France, the scientist Georges Cuvier established three races: white (Caucasian), black (Ethiopian), and yellow (Mongolian). This view became prevalent as a tolerant one.

CHAPTER 13

Culture is like light in a beautiful window, limited by the boundaries of decency.

The dawn of culture is a blessing for people. Living in peace and harmony is happiness.

On May 25, 2005, Liverpool and Milan faced off at the Olympic Stadium in Istanbul. The 2004/05 UEFA Champions League final, the 50th season in the history of the European Cup, was a historic, and unusual, match, judging by many factors. Liverpool miraculously won the penalty shootout despite trailing 3-0 in the first half. The drama that unfolded was incomprehensible. It wasn't just that Liverpool, led by Stevie Gerrard, scored three goals in the space of six or seven minutes in the second half . It wasn't that they managed to beat Milan on penalties. It's not that it was my favorite team's fifth Champions League title, and that it gave the club the opportunity to keep the trophy forever... The thing is, I'm a very passionate fan and have decades of experience watching heart-pounding games since 1974, and I suddenly decided to go home. We watched the match with my family at my parents' house, with my brother Nabi and son Alisher. Late at night, at 2 o'clock, just as the teams went for halftime, I said I was going home. No matter how much my son tried to persuade me and my brother asked me to stay, I was adamant. With a heavy heart, resentful of the team, forgetting about " You" ll Never Walk Alone ," I went home. And for the first time in my life, on the morning of May 26, 2005, I felt myself in some incomprehensible state. This feeling hadn't yet been given a name.

There are sports where men and women in many disciplines have the opportunity to compete fairly, representing their countries at the Olympics, world championships, continental championships, and other tournaments of all kinds. For its own survival, humanity must and must stop resolving issues through wars and other armed conflicts. First, it is necessary to conclude a memorandum on the media to monitor provocative accounts in print media and online social media, and to conduct ongoing UN monitoring of countries' education systems. All exposed provocateurs and disinformation agents sowing hostility along racial, ethnic, and religious lines must be subject to strict criminal prosecution, administrative fines, and community service.

To live in a prosperous world, peace must exist, first and foremost, in the soul, mind, feelings, and heart of every person. All human freedoms and rights must be balanced against obligations, and the same freedoms and rights of others must be respected without fail. Great countries have failed to live up to the value of being great by killing millions of civilians without trial or punishment for those found guilty of crimes, and by leaving civil servants who committed crimes against humanity without international judicial review. The status of "great" countries sitting on the UN Security Council must be abolished. The concepts of "great people," "great language," and all claims to being chosen by God must be abolished. We need to remind people more in all media that people descend from our forefather Adam and our foremother Eve, and that we are all definitely related.

CHAPTER 14

In life, everything is needed and necessary in its own time and place.

Everything has already been measured out and designated for each and everyone.

Our Prophet Muhammad, may Allah bless him and grant him peace, addressed young people and said: "O youth! Whoever among you is able to marry, let him marry." "Whoever is unable, let him fast." (Marriage means going against the tricks of the evil Satan.) In another hadith, he congratulated them: "May Allah grant you all His grace and unite you in goodness."

For example, in Islam there are no altars, idols, or statues, and therefore no priests or control centers. Each believer personally communicates directly and unilaterally with the Almighty God, repents of any sins they believe they have committed, consults on their intentions, and expresses gratitude for assistance rendered.

It must be stated: the Quran equates the murder of a human being with the murder of all humanity; it is a terrible sin, for which the murderer is promised eternal hell. In Islam, it is forbidden to force another person to convert to Islam. It is forbidden, haram. The divine Quran states: "There is no compulsion in faith..." These are mortal sins.

But what do we read in the media, what do nervous, uneducated historians write, what do political leaders say about Muslims , about Islam and Islamic culture in general?! Lies, deception, slander. This is blatant nonsense. For centuries, legends have been fabricated about how Islamist fanatics forced people to convert to Islam at knifepoint, and how those who remained faithful to the cross were killed by crucifixion. And this delirium of a clearly "cross-eyed gray mare" has been propagated from every angle for the past decades; the disinformation is shocking. And no one is held accountable. Zionism thrives in the media, parliaments, and courts. Having abolished Christianity, they have now begun to shake Islam.

Islam, above all, is freedom from the shackles of ignorance, a culture bound by love for the Most High God, Allah, the Holy and Great, and love for His best creation, Man. The manifestation of piety, the measure of all things, is the only way to receive Sawap (reward) from the angels for a noble deed. For the sake of the Pleasure of Allah the Most High and the effort to avoid by any means the manifestation of the Gunas that may cause the displeasure of Allah the Most High... In Islam, there are no informers, overseers, inspectors, gendarmes, everything is regulated by each believer in Allah... only within oneself critically, only on the basis of knowledge of the divine Quran (Sharia is an extract of laws and regulations on how and what should be done and decided when considering issues of affairs in certain cases of public life, we note that they are especially relevant and effective at all times) and the prophetic Sunnah (how the Prophet Muhammad, may Allah bless him and grant him peace, did, acted, advised, encouraged, and spoke edifications during his lifetime). When a believer has doubts, he asks a more knowledgeable fellow believer about the matter. If the question is related to the law or a difficult issue of fiqh of human rights or concerning social values, then this issue is considered by learned legal theologians and theosophists . Nowadays, these are usually muftis (Islamic countries organized according to the Christian worldview have appointed the heads of the confessions in the region) who issue a fatwa in accordance with the norms of Sharia.

It's worth noting here that courts in Christian-majority countries have outlived their usefulness and have demonstrated their limitations, as they judge in the name of the people. People, as we know, are prone to error. They can no longer cope with the volume and state of cases, even though the judicial corps is bloated beyond all reason. Jurisprudence in the US and Europe, like the circulatory system of a still-progressive part of the world, a country, or a state, is in a major traffic jam; the impassable gridlock of lawlessness and red tape staggers the imagination with its stagnation. But elites and societies try to ignore this, as long as it doesn't affect their interests.

The concept of the presumption of innocence now applies specifically only to unscrupulous, supposedly Christian rulers, nobles, bloodthirsty Zionists, and all bloodthirsty criminals, murderers, and rapists, but not to Muslims . This has taken on such forms and norms across the globe, including in countries where the population adheres to an Islamic worldview, a worldview previously reserved for Israel under its occupation regime. In the republics of the former USSR, the ruling puppets of Zionism have seemingly condemned citizens' piety, to the point of absurdity—here, men who pray are afraid to wear beards, and women are afraid to conceal their beauty with a hijab.

God-fearing, devout Muslims were innocently found guilty; millions of ordinary people in Iraq, Syria, Libya, Lebanon, and Afghanistan were killed by the armies of the Great Powers. They killed with all sorts of deadly weapons, just to kill more, despite the fact that these were civilians, children, women, and the elderly. Meanwhile, according to plans and orders from the military-industrial complex, experiments were conducted, comments and adjustments were made, and higher standards were set by testing new types of weapons on living people.

This was taken from the example of terrorist Israel, which for decades saved on expenses by testing new types of weapons on living people, rather than at testing grounds and laboratories.

There's a counterargument to this terrible evil. Global media regularly claim that organ transplants, cancer surgeries, and treatments are best performed in Israel. Okay, let's leave aside plastic surgery and cosmetic procedures. The very fact that there are no problems with donor organs, blood, bone marrow, or skin, and that pricing is so inexpensive and affordable for the average person in the US and Europe, is alarming. Where does all this come from in such volume and quantity?

In 2001, I was on a tourist trip to India. In Delhi, at the Taj Hotel, I met two young Jews from Russia at breakfast. I learned from them that they were involved in the procurement of donor organs from India to Israel, and that there were plenty of such agents here. Everyone was making easy money for bread and butter with a thick layer of black caviar. I remember hearing that prices had skyrocketed. The most interesting thing was that they were looking for donors in some newspaper.

Now, after the pre-planned provocation by the intelligence services involving the hostage taking of an Israeli soldier and the "Summer Rains" operation carried out in Gaza, it appears the agents will not be going to India for a long time.

Tens of millions of Muslims, having lost their honor and dignity, their home and property, became defenseless and despised refugees in Europe. Thousands were imprisoned in appalling conditions of abuse, languishing for years without trial in closed, specialized prisons, enduring torture and inhumane conditions. The Zionists didn't even spare their allies, the odious rulers in Islamic countries; they were murdered in the most blatant, vile, and despicable manner.

The fact that the so-called woman with the hyena smile admired these spectacles reinforces the impression of such pre-planned actions to intimidate the leaders of Islamic countries. But what a boost of courage and optimism was given to the frostbitten, sadistic psychopathic executioners Ariel Sharon, the Butcher of Beirut, and Benya Netanyahu, a master of systematic, bloody provocations involving harassment and humiliating moral and physical methods of intimidation of the peaceful Palestinian population, also the creator of Hamas—a select group of collaborators kept under surveillance by Israeli intelligence services, intended to negotiate agreements with them and create a corrupt mechanism for the equitable division of multi-billion dollar financial aid—as a counterweight to Yasser Arafat's PLO and the Fatah party.

"How is this possible? How can Hamas leaders kiss Netanyahu, even though there's still no state of Palestine? Recently, the maniac finance minister, resigning in protest against the withdrawal of Israeli settlements from the Gaza Strip, threatened to return and exterminate all its inhabitants, razing the concentration camp, that open-air prison, to the ground."

These and many other ghoulish Prime Ministers before them, all born in foreign countries, swore on the blood of a ritually slaughtered goat that they would never allow the establishment of a state of Palestine by the indigenous inhabitants of the Holy Land. If a glimmer of hope were to appear, a ray of light would break through the dark clouds, and the international community would decide to declare a state of Palestine, these scoundrels would have long since prepared a provocative plan. They would commit a terrorist attack surpassing the tragedy and death toll of September 11, 2001, and deliberately sacrifice 6,000-7,000 of their own Israeli citizens, and they would do so in such a way that foreigners, Muslims , and Christians would be among the victims.

It would be even better if the world's intelligence agencies supported the project of Netanyahu and his odious allies with bags of easy money - to create a mini-Islamic state somewhere nearby so that Islamic scholars and God-fearing families from all over the world could flock there to create a show of hell for the whole world to see.

Who would have doubted it?! Israel shook the foundations of Christianity in Europe, and in the US, with the introduction of liberal ideas and psychoanalysis, it abolished them. So, what's more important to a given American: Santa Claus, Valentine's Day,

Halloween, a psychoanalyst, or church? Somewhere, the collapse of the states looms like a terrifying specter. Therefore, the egghead politicians will soon be looking for a leader who's a fool with a rattle in his hand, so he can shake the air like a mad shaman with a drum.

In the US, partisan competition between Democrats and Republicans has long since ceased. Within the parties, factions and groups have become formalized, becoming the proverbial window dressing, creating the appearance of initiatives with debates and sham bargaining, while in reality, dividing up the spoils. The ideological struggle to improve the lives of American citizens has long been agreed upon and divided 50/50 between the blocs. The elites have merged to achieve Zionist goals. "About a Greater Israel in 51 states," they have essentially become friends in their shared interests and the sharing of spoils from a seemingly bottomless treasury. Some are on Olympus, others on Parnassus, living free from sorrow and worry, just as the famous Ivanushka the Fool dreams in Russian fairy tales – well-fed, drunk, and with their noses in tobacco (cocaine).

How was it possible in the United States, with its binding precedents, without a trial by jury, without an investigation, without witness testimony, and without mandatory evidence, to convict the Al-Qaeda organization led by Osama bin Laden and Mullah Omar of Afghanistan of the terrorist attack? Public opinion was intoxicated through its puppet media, with the notion that these main defendants had already partially admitted responsibility in several interviews with journalists. But these interviews contain not a hint of a confession; they are all available online. Another important claim is that the intelligence services allegedly have evidence: one of the suspects in the terrorist attack accidentally forgot his bag at the airport containing all the diagrams, maps, targets, and a list of the attack's participants. And everyone believed this nonsense; once again, the power of the media is in the hands of the Zionists.

For centuries, participants in court proceedings in developed countries have sworn on the Bible, even if they are not Christians.

Most of them not only don't understand the Holy Scriptures, but have never read them, remembering only fragmentary quotes from cartoons. The court, as an authority, exists on its own, having already become a political organ... Litigation, and generally everything related in any way to crime and legal disputes, has become an institution of juggling, a complex system of concepts... If all this were put together and imagined as a train carrying thousands of passengers, with its attendants, moving along the tracks according to a route and stopping at stations at precisely set dates and times when it is supposed to arrive, then everything here resembles Picasso's composition "Guernica," which expresses obstructive nonsense, although it was intended as a terrible indictment of fascism. So it is here. This speaks to one thing: sooner or later, the courts will have no choice but to admit their impotence in the face of the inability to resolve cases clearly, precisely, expeditiously, and, most importantly, understandably for all, according to the Law in the name of the Almighty God. A Sharia-based court would suit everyone. It is the most honest, fair, and efficient; there is no red tape, and it eliminates waste. The state and society are not burdened with the extraneous costs of maintaining prisoners in prisons and special facilities with security. Whether in criminal or civil court, everything is handled clearly, precisely, understandably for all, and, most importantly, in the shortest possible time. A suspect is held in a dungeon under guard only until the court's decision is rendered. After the trial, there is no detention of the guilty party in prisons or penal colonies.

Only a Sharia-compliant court never loses its full quality in the face of all the challenges of the times, for it is from God. Currently, humanity utilizes only a small portion of the capabilities of Sharia-compliant legal proceedings, limiting itself to: there is a prosecutor and a defense attorney. The prosecution and defense select jurors, necessarily an odd number, based on the principle that the larger the settlement, the larger the number, and that no one among them has an interest in the outcome of the case. The judge's authority was limited to pronouncing the court's verdict, based on the Divine Law and the jury's decision. Today, the justice system is consumed by red tape, empty talk, political creativity, and strategic and tactical maneuvers favoring the powerful, essentially transforming itself from a set of constructive indicators into a sacred instrument of international corruption. The litmus test for assessing the performance of the judicial system in all so-called Great Powers will be the answer "I don't believe it."

The formation of states based on the Islamic worldview, due to the presence of various religious movements and denominations within them, since their inception during the lifetime of the Prophet Muhammad (peace be upon him), necessarily included the Spiritual Administration of Religious Affairs. The religion of Islam, every Muslim in the state, undertakes the obligation to protect the interests of people of other religions. This was always clearly evident in the tax deductions of citizens in all Islamic countries: every representative of a different religion, whether local or visiting from other countries for trade or other reasons, paid the Jizya tax, which was always exactly half the tax paid by ordinary Muslims . This was done intentionally to create a favorable impression, to make the region attractive for business and, accordingly, to foster market competition. It also encouraged permanent relocation, the purchase or construction of real estate, and the creation of diasporas by non-Muslims, increasing the size and importance of the city. Moreover, let's not forget that Muslims also voluntarily paid Zakat annually, which amounted to 40% of their income, calculated independently to purify their wealth from greed. Every virtuous Muslim also contributed with compassion to the community life of their village, city, and country, by giving alms (sadaqah) to the suffering, the poor, the needy, the sick, and so on.

On the other hand, one cannot help but mention the unprecedented achievements of the human mind in culture and art, philosophy and medicine, technology and science. Muslims as individuals, and Islamic countries as states, developed the human mind and body in harmony according to Aristotle's kalokagathia .

has external beauty and internal virtue.

In society, in the hierarchy of the managers of small Jamaats and large ones of the many united Jamaats of Umms, only those persons who combine physical perfection and moral nobility should be represented.

But the philosophical minds of thousands of learned men never thought about the insidiousness that wars can be religious, and armies professional.

Essentially, this was the cause of the collapse and subsequent multitude of misfortunes, hardships, and deprivations of a thousand-year-old flourishing Islamic culture. Regression followed. Now the merits of Islam and Islamic culture are deliberately forgotten. They are in decline. They have been abolished in world history by the Zionists and their loyal lackeys—fanatics ignorant of religious matters, most of whom can be found, of course, among amateurish professing Christians, but in reality disguised atheists.

As the role of personal self-identification grew in multi-ethnic Europe, belonging to a nation, people, and faith became increasingly important. This became a catalyst for changing psychological types in social formations.

To study the stages of mass hypnosis instilled in a given population, to analyze the pernicious, deceitful, or rather distorted, mind of public opinion, suspended in a deep coma, it is necessary to establish measurement indicators. What do the authorities want? Why do they incite anger in the lumpen proletariat with hysterical outbursts? Everything will emerge and be seen.

The same thing is happening in Russia: a lot of raised voices, a lot of dissatisfaction. And the most interesting thing isn't the embezzlement of public funds by those in power, but Ukraine and Ukrainians. Everything became clear when propaganda, coupled with disinformation, took up the task and began stifling free speech with partial truths, and began relentlessly wielding the sabers of dubious arguments to tire and rape the defenseless, already confused, cerebral bodies of citizens of the former Soviet Union. Incidentally, the same approach is now being applied in the US and Europe to the crimes of bloodthirsty Zionists since 1948, almost 60 years ago.

To recreate even a relative sense of the spirit of that time of contradictions, we'll have to rewind the events of that time by a couple of years.

After the supposedly unexpected collapse of the Soviet Union, all and sundry of the countless wealth of social values somehow fell into Their hands. It 's no exaggeration to say that They destroyed the USSR. At this point, it's appropriate to apply the well-known saying: "I gave birth to you, and I will kill you." As is well known, They constituted 99% of the leadership and authorized figures of the All-Russian Central Executive Committee, the Russian Communist Party (Bolsheviks), and the All-Russian Extraordinary Commission.

Where it all began—I mean the process of divolution . Divolution (miracle—wonder and lucia —light), the process of "devilry in public opinion" that happened contrary to—that is, according to theory and logic, it shouldn't have happened. Everything is in the Will of Allah.

It all began with lies, with lies in the name of illusory mirages. This had happened more than once or twice. After an artificially created stalemate, the Union collapsed suddenly, unexpectedly for everyone, including the Zionists. They had only wanted to replace the old pillars with new ones, sturdy concrete walls that could have stood for decades, but the enormous palace, stuffed with untold riches, collapsed like a house of cards.

Now it's time for the collapse of the European Union, which is fragile in willpower, weak in front and behind, a lover of pleasure, pampered by the forbidden lust.

Then, of course, the inevitable collapse of the United States is inevitable, due to a civilian population dumbfounded by decades of scourging with the coding of doubts, handing over control of their destinies to deranged psychologists who supposedly know life and the world better. Of Them.

Systematic alcohol abuse in large quantities, especially strong drinks on Fridays, will definitely lead to stupefaction. The fact that selective approaches are observed everywhere is a symptom of the inevitability of collapse.

Rumors circulate that police officers occasionally arrest white boys for marijuana smoking, but pay no attention to black people... - What's the point? - Perhaps they're indifferent to the fate of African-American teenagers? Whatever the case, processes are ongoing in America, and all of them are depressing. LGBT, gender issues, school programs for gender identification, the destruction of the patriarchal family cult, with a deliberate tilt of laws and regulations toward matriarchy, formalism in the value interpretation of Faith and religion in general, all under the strict, watchful, and latent control of Orthodox Zionists and obscurantist Protestants. Wolves and sheep, completely ignorant of the Almighty God and knowledge of religion in general.

They were keenly aware of the winds of change and always kept their noses in the wind. They borrowed philosophical thinking from the Arabs, and how to control crowds of millions with lies, from the Popes. Have Satanists from all countries united?!

When, due to mass psychosis among ignorant fanatics, the Crusades of 1096–1204 to Palestine occurred. The alleged goal was to liberate the holy sites of Christianity.

The Crusades are a series of religious military campaigns launched by the Catholic Church against Muslims , pagans, and heretics from the kingdoms of Western Europe until the end of the 15th century. The primary goal was initially to conquer Jerusalem, supposedly home to the "Holy Sepulchre." In subsequent campaigns of conquest, while this has not been abolished to some extent, the primary goal, more broadly speaking, became not forced conversion to Christianity, but the desire to establish colonies of enslaved people, for the purpose of exploiting second-class citizens.

It should be noted that church indulgences were granted to tyrants, sadists, and marauders for murder, violence, and robbery, supposedly in the name of Christ.

Incomprehensible processes of dehumanization occurred in almost all countries of Christian Europe. Under Pope Innocent In 1215 , the Catholic Church created a special ecclesiastical court called the Inquisition, "the holy department for investigating heretical sins."

Now, the Zionists, having rebranded themselves as "destroying Islamic terrorism," have taken up arms and are leading a latent, hidden Crusade. Those with eyes see. Those with ears hear. Those with brains must take action. Zionism must be condemned and abolished. All international criminals must be held accountable for their crimes against humanity.

CHAPTER 15

Sanguine, Choleric, Phlegmatic, Melancholic—the supposedly classic temperaments, and a few other supposedly mixed types, and billions of variations with unstable, wandering bursts of psychotypes.... All of this is a convoluted phantasmagoria, a whim, a delusion based on one's own inner weakness, constitutional discomfort, inferiority due to ignorance of spiritual matters, and a multitude of doubts due to a lack of Faith and understanding of the Almighty God.

Vladivostok is a large city and port in the Russian Far East. November 2006, a foggy morning on the 23rd day with an unpleasant odor. Forecasters say the weather is unsuitable for flying for at least two weeks. I urgently need to get to Moscow. I'll have to take the train. Tickets are sold out, as expected. I had to rely on the resources of the Ministry of Defense's District Command. Accidental acquaintances are virtually unheard of, and I was once again convinced of this. A few days ago, I met Captain 1st Rank Alexander Valiev at the city hall. We then had a bite to eat at a restaurant during lunchtime, chatted about this and that, and exchanged phone numbers. The next day, we went fishing and had a wonderful day. We discovered common interests and shared opinions on many things.

And so, I have a ticket in my hand, even for a compartment, albeit for an upper berth. On my own, I couldn't even find a ticket for the next two or three days at exorbitant prices. But Sasha somehow got me one, and for today's flight, too.

I thanked my new friend heartily for his concern and care, wishing him all the best, good health, family happiness, and success in everything he could wish for. Finally, before bidding him a heartfelt farewell, I made him promise that if he ever came to Moscow, he would definitely let me know in advance of his arrival date.

The train had barely pulled into the platform when I was already at my car. I quickly stowed my suitcase and duffel bag in the overhead compartment and tucked in the bed linen. The compartment wasn't warm, but hot, and I was sweating all over. I'd barely changed into my tracksuit when a hugely built priest in a black fur coat, carrying large, swinging, jeweled gold crosses and thick chains, squeezed through the compartment door. His breath reeked of a distinctive, harsh, acrid fumes that filled the small space like an avalanche. He seemed oblivious to my greeting as I let him pass and then exited the compartment and headed down the corridor toward an open window.

Two plump priests in sheepskin coats were walking toward me, dragging two large suitcases. Behind them, three monks were dragging two enormous iron-lined chests. It occurred to me that they wouldn't fit in our compartment, when suddenly I saw the train conductor running from the other side of the car. From my compartment, I could hear the cursing of my fellow traveler, the priest, who was already beginning to lecture the train conductor. I decided to step onto the platform and get some fresh air; there were still 10-15 minutes before departure. In the vestibule, I helped a man in a long coat, glasses, and a cane into the car and drag his things.

I had just stepped onto the platform when night lamps began to come on everywhere, even though it was still light. Only now did the main mass of passengers appear, all in a hurry, searching for their cars, running with their luggage, rushing to take their seats. Cries of discontent, accompanied by obscenities from brutal men, and the grumbling and shrieking of women, came from everywhere. The loudest of all were the conductors. Their voices were in every key, all unpleasant in their nuanced meanings, especially the smoky falsetto.

The radio boomed with a hissing command for passengers to take their seats on the Vladivostok-Moscow train, signaling that the train was departing. I climbed into my car as well. A priest was waiting for me in the vestibule, dressed in a black Puma tracksuit , with gold crosses and chains, a black cap, and his right hand extended in greeting, his fingers adorned with enormous gold rings, sparkling with the purest diamonds and green emeralds. Shaking his hand, I told him my name. Without listening, he pulled me into a tight embrace. He then whispered frankly into my ear that he wouldn't remember my Eastern name, that his insides were melting from the alcohol he'd consumed over the past two days at the local diocese, for his farewell. He informed me that he was an archbishop and metropolitan, fifth in the hierarchy of the Russian Orthodox Church, or rather fourth, due to his powers, something I didn't understand. Anyway, he kept saying something in his fragrant voice right above my ear, so I began to slowly push him away. The drunken priest, to his credit, realized this; I realized he was still trying to control himself. Releasing me from his embrace, but still firmly squeezing my right hand, he introduced himself:

"They call me Father Timofey, Yakov Stepanovich in the world. You, my dear fellow, can call me Yashka or Stepanych. Anyway, my guts are burning, let's have a drink to get to know each other."

– Here I immediately answer him excitedly:

- Yakov Stepanovich... I didn't have time to buy alcohol, I was in a hurry to get to the train. A good man got a ticket three hours ago, God bless him.

"But the bishop did not let her finish and interrupted her mid-sentence.

- What are you talking about, my son? I have a whole arsenal of drinks in the compartment. I have everything.

– What do you like to drink? Vodka? Whiskey? Tequila?

- Maybe you prefer wine?

"Let's drink some Taiga vodka. The holy fathers sent me three two-liter decanters in a crate for the trip. No one in the world has ever tasted such goodness. It's medicinal, pure as a child's tear, and it contains viper's tongue, ginseng, and a sprig of red rhodiola. Listen, friend, come with me."

"We walked down the corridor and entered a compartment, and there on the bottom bunk, a man in glasses was working on a crossword puzzle. The same one I'd helped half an hour ago. He stood up, introduced himself as Vladimir Magomedov, and left the compartment, seeing the priest turn away and try to pull his suitcase out from under his bunk."

Finally, the bishop pulled out a leather suitcase and opened it on the table. The room was filled with the delicious aromas of smoked meats: meat, sausage, fish, all sorts, even though they were all vacuum-packed. The priest placed one package of each type in the bag, then, looking around, said,

"You're probably a Muslim. You can safely eat all kosher food. You and everyone else are allowed to consume it. As is well known, Jews don't eat pork. These treats were brought from Jerusalem by a pilgrim monk. Everything is made according to the famous recipes of the hospitable Philistines, created many centuries ago. This is a classic of the history of taste."

My dear friend, go ahead and take this bag and head to the restaurant. I'll go for a quick drink now, then I'll come back to you with a decanter. Let's have a glass of this balm. Come on, get yourself a good seat.

- When I was walking down the corridor, Vladimir, who was standing by the open window, stopped me.

"Don't blame me, I left you so quickly. The fat priest there didn't even want to return my greeting or introduce himself. I stood there with my hand outstretched, but he simply turned away. I left to avoid being rude, I was in a hurry and passed right past you."

"Don't be upset, brother. There was no malice involved. Your name is Vladimir, and mine is Rakhman. You have a beautiful last name, I appreciate that."

"I tried to skillfully change the subject of the conversation, but Vladimir turned everything completely to nowhere.

"Rahman, you have a beautiful name; it goes perfectly with my last name. It wouldn't hurt to have a drink for that. It's a week's drive to Moscow, so fellow travelers should always maintain a pleasant atmosphere in their conversations. Something special happened in my life; I distinguished myself in an important matter, and now I might get a medal. Well, they'll give me a pretty penny, that's for sure. Anyway, I passed the tests of my torpedo at the Pacific base's range with flying colors. We celebrated our success with vodka for a few days. Now I'm feeling under the weather, so I need a drink immediately."

- I already opened my mouth to answer, but he extended his hand to my face as if gesturing that no unnecessary words were needed.

"Rahman, brother. I have drinks and snacks for every taste. Rear Admiral Arkady, nicknamed Gnus, personally supplied me with supplies for the journey. It's all there."

- What are you going to drink? What am I even asking? Brother, go to the restaurant, I'll grab everything and come over to you, just be bored for a minute.

"I was very surprised by the menu in the restaurant. Or rather, shocked. There was no food, absolutely nothing. The only choices were instant noodles, mashed potatoes, dry soups—all the usual Chinese staples. In other words, inedible. And tea, coffee, and jelly in bags. The dining car was empty, save for two guys of a certain appearance with tattoos on their arms, playing cards.

A waiter in a white chef's hat approached the table and asked what I wanted to order. At that moment, the door swung open noisily, and Vladimir appeared, holding a bag. Behind him, a heavy-set archimandrite, his powerful chest thrust forward, walked. I left the table and first sat Vladimir down, then took a large greenish decanter from the priest's hands, saying,

- Here is your personal, best place, dear Yakov Stepanovich!

"I invited them to sit at one side of the Metropolitan's table. I first introduced them to each other with ornamental observations, laced with humor. But the priest interrupted me with a curt order, attempting to immediately claim authority."

- My son, open the decanter. Pour everyone a full glass and say a toast.

- Here a learned man intervened in the conversation.

- You, Yakov Stepanovich, are not in church now, but in a restaurant. First, we must say two words: what will we drink – vodka or cognac? I'll have Hennessy cognac. I brought a liter, there's another one in the compartment. I'm saying this in case we suddenly get an appetite, knowing there's another one. - Do you think mixing alcohol is more expensive?!

- But here the priest spoke in an unexpectedly open bass voice.

- My dear fellow. You are sitting at the same table and traveling in the same compartment with an archbishop... a metropolitan... a vicar... fifth in the hierarchy of the Holy Church. But perhaps fourth in terms of available opportunities in the Old Russian Orthodox Church, so I ask you, cabin boy, to entrust me, your holy father, to be the captain of our submarine. I am concerned about your stomachs.

God sent us a healing potion that truly heals and does not harm.

– At the end of his speech, he pointed his finger at a large glass decanter, beautifully shimmering with transparency like a strange aquarium, in which a snake froze, coiled as if preparing to jump, among the bushes of roots and leaves.

We drank to our acquaintance after the first general toast, where everyone had the opportunity to express their feelings and opinions. The fragrant brew had a certain aftertaste and went down smoothly, like oil, but it wasn't disgusting.

We snacked on meat delicacies from Jerusalem with rice bread and soy sauce. We washed it down with Borjomi mineral water and a delicious homemade lemonade from the local bishop's local diocese, as a distinguished fellow traveler told us. We didn't understand anything, but thanked everyone who had prepared the drink. The scholar busily put the cognac in a bag, uttering the magical "we'll drink later," then proposed a toast to "a successful trip and an easy journey" and began pouring a little more than half a glass of vodka into everyone's 100-gram shot glasses, starting with the bishop. But the priest ordered that they drink fully to the second toast; from the third toast onward, they could regulate their drinking. We poured the full glass, drank, and ate.

Vladimir Magomedov, a doctor of technical sciences, pulled fried cutlets and seaweed salads from his bag. Then he called the waiter over and ordered strong black tea, suggesting everyone drink hot tea to maintain balance. We, of course, agreed. Then I couldn't resist, either, and under the pretext of needing to use the restroom, I went back to my compartment. I didn't return empty-handed. I grabbed some rye bread, a liter jar of fresh red caviar, a pack of New Zealand butter, a dozen boiled eggs, and a box of fresh Ptichye Moloko chocolates. All for tea.

My neighbors' delight is hard to describe; their emotions were off the charts. "Perhaps it was a friendly prank?" The Metropolitan was particularly enthusiastic in his drunken stupor. He snorted loudly, opened a jar of caviar, scooped it up with a tablespoon, and hurriedly tasted it. He closed his eyes in bliss and declared:

"It was ecstasy, I almost came from pleasure... The eggs burst in my mouth like fireworks." Then, reading the name of the Red October confectionery factory on the box of chocolates, he said in a drawn-out voice, kissing her:

- My be - loved ones ! And the release date, they're only four days old. Well, my friend, what was your name again? Sorry, your names are so hard to remember. I'm afraid of getting it wrong.

- Vladimir intervened, showing off his erudition.

- Actually, it would be correct to call our friend. It would be more correct to call him brother.

Abdurakhman, not Rahman. What does "slave of the Merciful Allah" mean? Moreover, it turns out he's a man of great spirit, a natural diplomat; everything he does in dealing with people comes naturally to him. It's obvious. Look how kind the waiter is to him. He also helped me, a stranger, when we first met... And he introduced us, after all. So I propose a toast to our brother, probably the youngest. What year were you born, Yakov Stepanovich?

- I'm fifty-three. It will be tomorrow. God willing.

"He blurted out the words like a howitzer firing, with pauses and pauses, and at the end of his speech, the priest crossed himself without getting up. Then he yawned widely, then crossed his mouth. After a brief silence, he turned to the barmaid, who was passing by, pushing a trolley loaded with all sorts of things, cigarettes, pastries, and various canned goods.

"My daughter, run and call that idiot, the King of Heaven, the train conductor. If he doesn't want trouble, let him come quickly. Tell him the Holy Father is angry."

"The young woman paused for a moment, lost in thought. Then he softly rapped his knuckles on the table, his eyes narrowed sternly, and quietly muttered a threat:

- You're still here? And you want problems?

– The woman, leaving her goods, ran to look for her boss.

CHAPTER 16

Death is like going into oblivion, forever. This is

when you are no longer in this world. There is nothing left.

cannot be changed or fixed. All the pain is behind us,

there is uncertainty ahead...

The train conductor ran into the dining car, adjusting his uniform and cap as he went. He stood at the table and stood at attention. A breathless barmaid ran after him and also stood at his side, subservient . Both of them had flushed faces, their eyes darting back and forth in fear. They stood frozen, rooted to the spot.

The priest began to scold the girl first.

- Are you a barmaid, a member of the service staff? That cloth kokoshnik on your head and that white robe have darkened, become almost gray. Aren't you ashamed? - You're a woman, aren't you?! Go and tidy yourself up. Get a couple of hours' sleep, rest. Wash yourself thoroughly here and there, comb your hair, and put on some perfume and deodorant. In short, dress like you're going on a date. And I'll expect you in three hours; you can look after us and the table.

Bring two sheets right now. Then you're free. - Do you understand everything?

"It was hard to look at the girl. She stood there, blinking rapidly, looking from us to her superior. The archbishop asked quietly.

- What's the matter? Are you stupid or something? Go and do your job.

- The barmaid, seeing that her boss was silent, quietly said in a plaintive voice:

"Father, I have a sales plan. I need to sell and look after the passengers. We just left... I have a one-year-old son to raise and my parents to help. I divorced my husband three months ago, and now we're living with my parents; we need the money. And... We..."

- The priest did not listen to her.

- You'll tell me about this tomorrow night, when I absolve you of your sins. - You've probably accumulated them already? You're probably sinning with just anyone? Well, go ahead and go. Remember one thing - we're passengers too. Important and necessary.

"The bishop pulled a pile of folded dollar bills from his pocket, pulled out five or six bills, folded them in quarters, and stuffed them into the gap in her chest between two melons. The girl ran to carry out the order." Without wasting any time, he began criticizing his superior.

"You hold such an important position, you idiot, boss. The country has entrusted you with a part of itself stretching for thousands of kilometers." "And what are you doing? You've only just set out, you're transporting people, not brainless cattle..." "Why is your uniform wrinkled and stained? Did you spend the night in a barn or something? The peak of your cap is faded... And the hairs are sticking out of your nose... Where did they find you freaks? Who trusted you to run the train? There are thousands of people here: old people, women, small children... You idiots will ruin the country. Wherever you spit, there are problems, and where there's nothing, there's always trouble..."

— At that moment, the barmaid rushed in, wearing a new cap and robe, with two new sheets in her hand. The bishop commanded:

"Give it to the boss, he'll cover our table on both sides so we don't disturb people with our feast. I don't want to be a thorn in people's side on my birthday. They'll go crazy with us being so fat here. What's your name, child? How old are you, Freckles?"

"The embarrassed girl answered with a smile.

- Aglaya Petrovna Butusova. I'm twenty-five years old.

- The Metropolitan nodded his head.

"You can go and rest. Return to work in two hours and 40 minutes. Clear the table of unnecessary items. Make sure we eat and drink, and keep our plates clean. You need to keep an eye on us and the people around us at all times, to make sure nothing goes wrong; there are all sorts of people around here."

The priest turned to face the table where two shaggy Gavroches were playing cards. They, hearing the barbed words, paused their game and also turned to face us. Then he said to the chief:

- Who are these? - Have you opened a mobile casino on the tracks? - Maybe there are prostitutes on the train? - Answer me, you unfortunate man.

It was impossible to look at the train conductor indifferently. He stood there looking miserable, lost, as if he'd shrunk. Then he came to his senses, straightened his cap, and addressed the gamblers loudly:

- Show your documents and travel tickets. - Answer when asked: "Who gave you permission to gamble in a public place?"

Two middle-aged men, undoubtedly experienced and well-traveled, having tasted more than a few pounds of bitter salt, pretended to bustle about. Then, pulling leather wallets from their jacket pockets, they took out the requested items and placed them on the table. Approaching their table, a tall man in a peaked cap and striped suit introduced himself with a businesslike, stern air:

- Train conductor Maxim Fedorovich Sutuly. With whom do I have the honor of speaking?

So. Bastrykin Panteley Emelyanovich. It's you. You're going to Chita. So that's clear. 35 years old. Single? 36 soon and single. Yeah, right.

So. Spiridonov Semyon Stepanovich. Three SSS. Also in Chita. You're going to a friend's birthday. Such a long way. Such buddies, I understand. Also single. What a fashion it is. Some don't get married, others get divorced. Not life, but a crossword puzzle with outrage. Everything seems normal. You also remember, you can't break the rules. There are people around. You're disturbing the peace with your card games. People are eating here, it's a public place.

- The bishop intervened in the conversation, where only the voice of the train conductor was heard.

- Everyone come here. Quickly. Boss, stand here and see how you're supposed to be hanging out with them. Listen up, guys. You've got the official seal of approval on your foreheads; you've probably each had two or three stints under your belt? Why aren't we talking? Why don't you at least nod? So keep quiet, we'll keep quiet. If you want trouble, I see, I can give you another prison sentence if you insist... This is the last time I'll ask: do you have any criminal records? - Who, and how many?

- The gangster-like thugs both raised their hands. Then, in turn, each one briefly reported to the stern censor.

- Semyon Stepanovich Spiridonov. Convicted twice. For hooliganism and theft.

"What did you steal?" the priest asked the sturdy man, rising and leaving the table.

"At TsUM, the director's safe was broken into just before New Year's, and there were only pennies in it. The Georgian director stole it all before us. Then they pinned the millions on us."

"No one expected what happened. The Metropolitan thrust his left hand straight into the interrogator's stomach. He cried out in surprise, bent forward slightly, and was then struck by a powerful blow from above. The man, named Semyon, was knocked out cold. The priest explained himself briefly.

"I beg your pardon, gentlemen comrades, I couldn't resist. I don't like lies. He has murderer written all over his forehead. Someone like him won't be too soft-spoken or dirty his hands with theft. Only people like him are capable of murder, rape, and, of course, robbery and blackmail."

- So what? - Am I right? - the priest asked another man being interrogated, wiping his hands with a napkin.

- No, I don't know. Father, we met two hours ago.

"This thin man of average height didn't have time to finish his sentence; on the last syllable, he was struck by a precise, short left kick to the liver. Another knockout. The bishop ordered the train conductor to conduct a search and draw up a report. He called two passengers, restaurant patrons who had been unintentionally caught up in the brawl, to act as witnesses. Then he said he needed to go to the restroom to wash his hands. Crossing himself, he turned to Vladimir and me.

- My friends, brothers. You too, go wash up and come back quickly. You'll probably be surprised, but such things happen here in Mother Russia. Constantly extreme. The same thing. Stole, drank, went to prison. Robbery, violence, the scaffold. Romance.

The chief arrived with two assistants and began searching the pockets of the motionless bodies, seemingly asleep, which had aroused the passengers' suspicions. Vladimir and I also rose from the table and followed the priest to tidy ourselves up, and of course, our thoughts.

The emotions from what I saw were off the charts.

About twenty minutes later we met him in the vestibule; he was standing there, deep in thought and smoking. Next to him, a plump girl of about 15-16 years old was smoking and talking animatedly and laughing on the phone, stamping her feet and screaming emotionally from all sorts of apparently pleasant news coming from afar.

My friend pulled out a pack of classic Marlboros and opened the box. I politely declined. Two more women entered the vestibule and also lit up happily, chatting nonstop. Vladimir abruptly stubbed out his cigarette and tossed the butt into a large, lidded ashtray screwed to the side of the car.

We passed through two compartment cars and reached the dining car; our end table was already neatly curtained with sheets, and from there we could quietly hear the voice of our priest.

We approached a reserved area separated from the restaurant, and my friend, coughing loudly for decency, said:

- Yakov Stepanovich, we are here, can we come in?

- What are you talking about? Of course, come in, I've been waiting for you for a long time. Look what's going on here?

ADIDAS tracksuit. and spoke on a gold Vertu cell phone With someone. Our friend, displaying remarkable gestures, managed to apologize for his chatter and asked me to pour vodka into shot glasses, put some appetizers on plates, and prepare to make a toast. I proposed a toast to the parents. Everyone liked the toast and drank deeply. We learned that during the search, approximately sixty thousand US dollars, a Finnish knife, and brass knuckles were found on the men. That they were currently bound hand and foot in a compartment in the next train car, and that tomorrow at lunchtime they would be met by a police squad and two detectives from the Khabarovsk Criminal Investigation Department. At the end of his story, the priest confidently declared, summing up:

- My dear brothers. I tell you for sure, here's the holy cross (he crossed himself three times). They committed some kind of robbery in Vladivostok. In Khabarovsk, the detectives will quickly search their compartment and find some other evidence in their belongings. You'll see it for sure.

- At that moment, someone stamped their feet loudly behind the curtains made of sheets.

"Come in, my son," the Metropolitan permitted. A monk with long blond hair, a large iron cross on a thick black thread, and a black cassock entered, a giant of enormous stature who had brought us a small television with antennas. He was so attentive to the words spoken by the archbishop, standing at attention, ready to carry out any order, that from an outsider it seemed highly abnormal, fanatical, and perhaps even dangerous. It was clear, of course, that the monk was mute, but his animal-like devotion to the bishop, coupled with his brazen, ostentatious disrespect for those around him and his hidden aggression, somehow made one nervous. And his gaze, from under his eyebrows, was superficial, soulless, as if he were looking at inanimate objects. Vladimir remarked on this to me later in our conversation.

The priest ordered the monk to bring the gifts given to him by the holy fathers on behalf of the ruling bishop of the diocese for the long journey. He explained that everything would need to be examined, sorted, and stored separately, for tomorrow was the feast day of his appearance in the world of God, and he needed to partake of the delicacies and refreshments with the guests, and offer thanks for the generous tokens of affection sent to his brothers in Christ.

CHAPTER 17

Islam is the religion of Allah, expressed in submission to God's laws, dedication to the faith of the One God, His messengers and following the precepts of the Holy Quran, the Sunnah of the Prophet Muhammad, in prayers, virtue, charity, improvement of knowledge, spirituality and physicality.

A Muslim is a devoted follower of Monotheism, a person who has submitted to Allah the Most High, believed in the Law of God, and accepted Islam, a jinn.

Iman is the acceptance by the heart of the truth of Islam, faith in the One Allah, His angels, His Scriptures (the Quran, Torah, Zabur/Psalms, Injil/Gospel), His prophets (Muhammad and others. Peace be upon them), the Day of Judgment/Day of Resurrection, the predestination of everything from Allah: good and evil.

A Mu'min is someone who sincerely believes in Allah; faith is the meaning of their life, influencing the nobility of their thoughts and actions. A Mu'min's level of Monotheism is one step higher than that of a Muslim.

Ihsan is the highest level of faith and virtue in Islam, when a Muslim worships Allah Almighty with the awareness of a constant spiritual connection, that God always sees them, the highest level of sincerity and understanding of the religion of Monotheism. It is the pursuit of perfection of feelings and reason, the attainment of ultimate beauty in sincerity of intentions and piety in all actions in earthly life.

Muhsin is the highest level of orthodoxy (achievable by anyone in monotheism), a unique understanding of the One God: Almighty,

Eternal, Compassionate, Merciful, Lord of time and space, Truth and Absolute, Whom all created by Him need, but who needs no one; if He wills something, He says, "Be it," and it is. It is perhaps the mystical essence of personal development, with the erasure of all earthly materialism and social mores from the mind and emotions. Its highest value is benevolence toward all without exception, beneficence expressed through charity, asceticism, and modesty.

You should live easily, freely, without unnecessary strain, even when experiencing difficulties and adversity. Everything is clear and understandable to you. Don't lose focus, measure everything in terms of magnitude, preferably large ones, so you can move in the right direction. Where is right and where is wrong is another matter entirely. You must search with your heart and mind. You can't rely on trivial circumstances, as Zionists and idle atheists tend to do, for in them you can easily become confused, lose your rhythm, and lose your bearings.

We must be strong and endure this. God sends us troubles and misfortunes to find out who is who. – What can we compare this to in life? Exactly.

- The bishop raised his glass and clinked it with us, drinking without eating.

"You know Palestine and the people descended from the Philistines who live in the Holy Land, where the tombs of our forefather Adam and our foremother Eve are located, and where many holy prophets, beginning with Abraham, rest." (The bishop stood and crossed himself three times.) "This people has been pious since ancient times. Their faith is hidden not in their hearts, not in their minds, but in their blood. From ancient times, they have welcomed pilgrims from all over the world and ascetics who repented of the abundance of sins and who embarked on the straight path of Orthodoxy. And this people of God, like little children, is punished in their fate by the scourge of selfish hypocrites who betrayed God's law for thirty pieces of silver."

The dumb Anglo-Saxons plotted to use the Jews in their predatory plans to conquer the infidels in the Middle East. They coveted their bankrolls, thinking they would finance their New Crusade so they could seize the untold riches of the Arabs and Persians. They thought they'd cut off a slice of the Holy Land and then kiss their asses. But that wasn't the case. Their chicken-brains won't be able to cope with the Zionists. They have cannibalistic loan sharks behind them, television and radio 24/7, the internet and newspapers, all those crooked, lying, corrupt journalists, lawyers, judges, prosecutors, customs, Interpol, all the world's intelligence agencies are bought outright, all the terrorists work for them, all the scum and dirt: crooks, thieves, spies, drug addicts, and prostitutes. Everyone and everything is in their sweaty hands. All the filth of demons, basically. All members of one circle and the circle of one member, a party called Corruption.

Without consulting the hundreds of thousands of people who lived righteously with God's name on their lips from early morning until late at night, they suddenly, in one fell swoop, settled tens of thousands of refugees among them, along with a demonic people who had been swindling for millennia... Christ-sellers. Essentially, it's like introducing a parasitic goat into a cabbage patch. No, it would be better to say, like introducing a full-grown, hungry wolf into a sheepfold...

What does homeland mean? It's like the song says. Where were you born, the land where you grew up, went to school, lived among family and loved ones, where are your friends, where are the ashes of your fathers and grandfathers? And then they set a trap, and everyone is lying. And those who decided all these questions received glory, honor, immortalization in world history, and material wealth.

Two thousand years after the Romans expelled these Golden Calf worshippers, the new micro-Caesars resettled not Sephardic Jews, but the descendants of the Ashkenazi Khazars, whose distant ancestors supposedly converted to Judaism. They aren't even Jews, after all, just a hodgepodge of sedentary Gypsies and all the nomadic peoples on the highway. According to historical justice, the most shameless people are the inhabitants of Sodom and Gomorrah, who have no concept of honor or conscience. Honestly, you hear it said in all the books of Holy Scripture. (The tipsy priest stood up and crossed himself three times.) And what were those damned people thinking? It's incomprehensible.

The Philistines are like little children to these thugs, much less a people accustomed to lying. They've been so tormented by these monsters for six decades, tortured, tormented, and subjected to daily abuse. They stole everything: mountains, land, water, gardens, sea, fields, even the air of freedom. They drove them from their homes, stole the homeland of several million, and killed over a million. And now they kill every day, especially children. We Christians have allowed this unthinkable atrocity. They tortured and tormented the people of Christ, whose Son of God they tortured, forced Pontius Pilate to crucify the Messiah, and persecuted his followers. This is clearly the will of Satan.

How was this possible? A people who supposedly suffered the fate of slavery, endured genocide and the Holocaust, is now pursuing a policy of scorching the land of indigenous peoples, erasing their history... The worst part is, these are their cousins.

So, the atheists, the godless worshippers of the notorious Satan, in order to eradicate the Orthodox faith and the belief in the One God, in the Holy Trinity, have invented, with the help of the fornication of obscurantist fantasies: atheism, communism, fascism, Zionism, instilling all sorts of ideas and thoughts into the minds of people, in order to ultimately abolish the concept of monotheism.

"There's no point in hiding it, so far they've succeeded. Everything is moving according to Satan's plan; humanity is slowly, slowly sliding down the hill of orthodoxy to the brink of the permissive abyss of unbelief."

Everything is moving slowly and surely toward a major war, not the kind the Zionists have planned, for Christians to kill Muslims, but one in which, after millions of Muslims have been killed, it is Christians who will unleash their wrath against the parasitic Jews. Then there will be lengthy trials, and scientists will wash the bones of the murdered and identify their names. The trial of the murderers will end, and the real war will begin, a battle between believers in the Lord God and the atheists, consumers of bloody scenes, living for today.

It is Muslims who prevent this flood of pus and feces from overflowing. We contemptuously call them infidels, but they are a hard-working people. They have clear minds, generous hearts, pure souls, and skillful hands. A people who have learned the knowledge of the Power of the Almighty God from their mother's milk will never follow the temptations of a fallen angel. They may stray a little, but soon they will see the light, return, repent before the All-Forgiving Allah, and live on, improving the traditions of Monotheism.

Yesterday, I was sharing my thoughts with the holy fathers after their concerns about the infidels who have arrived in the Far East with their families. They're building, sowing, engaging in various businesses, opening markets and trading skillfully... I'm speaking to the elders... Address the laity, tell them not to worry about these people; they're closer to us than the Chinese, let them put down roots and settle down. These are God's people, they have knowledge of Monotheism, their tomorrow is theirs, they will always follow God's word. Their greatness lies in their ability to believe. What we ourselves have lost...

- At that moment, someone coughed behind the curtain and a pleasant female voice asked,

- Can I come in to see you, Father?

- Come in, daughter, you are welcome. - Who are you?

We recognized the beautiful young woman as the barmaid. The archbishop amazed everyone with his phenomenal memory.

- And that's what you are... Aglaya Petrovna Butusova! Blood and milk, and cheeks with dimples. All natural, no deception. You made this day a little more beautiful. Live and be healthy, find yourself happiness on the crest of success... I see. Bless you. God! Okay, listen. We're all going to go away for half an hour or an hour. You clean up here, set the table with a white tablecloth. If by any chance the head chef doesn't have a white tablecloth, tell your brother monk Gregory, he'll dig one up from under the ground and bring it to you. Don't doubt it. He may be mute, but he's a smart man.

He's currently sorting out the meat, poultry, and fish, all sorts of pies, mushrooms, and pickles. You should set the table with a womanly, tasteful air. We'll have a quick drink and then get ready for the celebration. In two hours and thirty-seven minutes (the bishop glanced at the dial of his gold Rolex with its sparkling diamonds), my family and friends will begin congratulating me on my birth. The Patriarch might pay his special attention if the Vicar Metropolitan reminds me... The Holy Fathers might call... And I'm expecting a call from our Tsar, Vladimir Vladimirovich, at the Presidential Administration. So I'll go get dressed in light colors.

You, my dear friends and brothers , wouldn't hurt to change your clothes for suits, too. Movement is life, and much movement is longevity. A holiday is when everyone's soul is light and comfortable, everyone is well-fed and happy with life. Not like the Jews, where it's all just me, me, me. Come on, Vladimir, pour me a drink, I have a toast, it's ready.

So, last year, we were with a holy brotherhood of Orthodox pilgrims in the Holy Land of Palestine. After visiting the Church of the Holy Sepulchre, viewing Golgotha, the Stone of Anointing, the Via Dolorosa (the Way of the Cross of Jesus Christ), the Mount of Olives in Gethsemane, the Upper Room of the Last Supper on Mount Zion, King David's Tomb, then the Church of the Nativity in Bethlehem, and then the city of Jericho, I suggested that, despite their fatigue, the pilgrims head to the ancient church of St. Porphyrius of Jerusalem, an Orthodox church in Gaza City. The church is located in the Zaytun neighborhood of Gaza's Old City, a predominantly Sunni Muslim community. There aren't many Christians among the Palestinians there; whether there will be a thousand Orthodox Christians or not is unknown.

"So, what was I talking about?" I almost lost my train of thought. Anyway, what struck us wasn't this ancient history, nor these holy sites, shrouded in legends of the Crusader knights. Rumor has it that they built this church in the 12th century, on the site of an older one erected in the 5th century by Saint Porphyry himself. Incidentally, his tomb is also located there, in the eastern corner of the church.

We were shocked by the appalling conditions of poverty and complete dependence on the Israelis in which the Palestinians live. It's a vast prison, or rather, an open-air ghetto-concentration camp. Everything is visible and audible, everything is visible and eavesdropped on. Along the entire perimeter of Gaza is a high fence with observation posts with floodlights every 300-350 meters, manned by sentries armed with machine guns and all sorts of weapons. All the fences are equipped with audio, video, and motion sensors; they say not a mouse could get through.

The Americans have invested the most modern special equipment and billions of dollars to intensify the oppression of the disenfranchised indigenous people of Palestine. And what experience do they have in history? They have exterminated tens of millions of indigenous Indians.

At the slightest mishap, the electricity, water, and gas are cut off, because everything is controlled and managed from the outside—from the Israeli Prime Minister's office, ministers, Knesset committees, the intelligence services, the Ministry of Defense, and so on and so forth. In short, two and a half million residents are truly hostages, without any right to free expression, without any human rights. They now have only one way to gain freedom: death.

And you know what makes me indignant? "Why is this entire nation being punished?" "Why doesn't the whole world care about this disgrace in the 21st century? Have the Zionists forgotten the Holocaust? And anyway, if they're demonstratively committing genocide, then everything's incomprehensible... It turns out that Zionism and fascism are murderous brothers in misfortune. Moreover, Zionism is far more terrifying; it acts based on existing experience, meaning it tortures with expertise. And anyway, it's all about money; Zionism is the father of corruption.

They have numerous security services, and any one of these government agencies can turn off the lights, water, and gas. They can launch a missile or drop a bomb on supposed terrorists at any moment. These people have lived under a "perpetual" curfew for generations; after 5 p.m., they're not allowed to leave their homes without permission from the Israeli authorities. They even have shock therapy, supposedly used as a preventative measure. From time to time, surprise raids are carried out by numerous units to penetrate deep into Gaza and cause a stir: checking documents, demolishing buildings if the walls aren't up to standard, investigating for signs of tunnels, and arresting suspicious individuals.

So even this multi-layered security system isn't enough for them. Now, reconnaissance planes are flying overhead, meticulously taking photos, recently gifted to them by the US. Furthermore, they allegedly maintain a huge paid network of informants from Palestinian collaborators, employing around two thousand people. Now imagine how many tens of thousands of prison guards, brought in from all over the world, are keeping an eye on the prisoners, natives of the Holy Land, imprisoned in Gaza? This is blatant blasphemy. A crime.

Israeli intelligence services monitor the world, collecting any information of interest. IDF troops constantly conduct localized military operations outside Israel's borders, attacking and killing civilians in neighboring states. At Israel's behest, the US regularly wages wars in the Middle East.

And all these refugees—not Semites, but millions of half-breed Ashkenazi Jews, pork-eating, vodka-drinking, drug-using, and sex-obsessed Jews—gathered from all over the world in Israel, are living off the American people, receiving allowances, salaries, and bonuses. The United States supplies them with the most advanced offensive weapons, including airplanes, missiles, and bombs, free of charge. Billions of dollars in additional financial aid are constantly being injected into their systems every month. An aircraft carrier is constantly on patrol in the ocean.

Israel also receives its entire pension fund from there. Since 1948, the United States has spent trillions of dollars on the Palestinian genocide. And for these astronomical gifts, the American people have received nothing but condemnation from many countries for their complicity in the crimes of murdering innocent civilians and curses from the nations subjected to treacherous attacks. Zionists claim that life is painful and commit terrible acts.

So, there you have it. Despite everything, the children, seeing us from afar, recognized us as guests and ran towards us from all sides. Some brought bread, some olives, some water and cheese. I even burst into tears. In short, let's drink to these God-given people.

CHAPTER 18

The Almighty God gave the Law to the forefather Adam, the prophet Nuh (Noah) and the prophet Ibrahim (Abraham).

He revealed the Tablets to Prophet Musa (Moses), the Gospel to Isa (Jesus), and the Quran to Prophet Muhammad. Peace be upon all the prophets and blessings until the Day of Judgment.

Jews adhere to the Torah, Christians to the Gospel, Muslims to the Quran—all supposedly believe in the One God. But strangely, the entire world of monotheists always lives by the laws of atheists and Satanists.

The Archbishop was dressed in his festive travel attire with the help of three monks in the Chief of the Train's compartment.

Vladimir Adamovich Magomedov, an Avar by nationality as it turned out, and I took turns changing clothes in our compartment, using plenty of wet and dry wipes. An hour or so later, fresh and completely sober, we stood in the dining car, wearing light-colored shirts without ties, formal suits, and chic shoes. Vladimir even had elegant cufflinks on his shirt cuffs. We kept a watchful eye on the bustle, with the small, unnecessary movements of hands in medical gloves—the so-called creative work of the girl Aglaya—as we awaited the arrival of the Metropolitan.

Finally, dressed in all the solemn, festive vestments of a bishop and his monastic habit, the priest of the highest rank appeared, accompanied by three monks. They escorted the Metropolitan to us, kissed his hands, and sat down at the end table.

He first greeted several people dining in the restaurant, then asked us to sit down at a table decorated with all sorts of exquisite dishes and piled high with all sorts of delicacies, in the corner of which stood a new decanter of vodka with a snake and two bottles of French champagne.

One of the monks brought him a silver vessel with a small aspergillum, and our familiar giant, Gregory, brought a smoking censer. The priest muttered some incantations and began sprinkling holy water around with the whisk, while the mute monk began pacing back and forth, swinging the censer. A few minutes later, three monks began assisting the priest in removing all of his episcopal vestments. First, the miter was removed from his head, then the vestments: the sakkos, omophorion, and panagia. Finally, with a show of respect, they removed the staff from his hand.

The archbishop didn't remain in his riding breeches and white long-sleeved shirt for long; soon, a lame monk brought him a khaki wool frock coat with a stand-up collar and helped him dress. The priest thanked his assistants for their attention with a wondrous collection of archaic words. Then, taking a large tray of roasted duck-like poultry from a side table, topped it with a dark rye pie with Far Eastern berries and pineapple, he handed it to the mute monk with a few words.

- Have some tea, brothers, tomorrow, if you can, don't fast.

"He began to cross them and everyone else in the carriage. When the monks left, he came up to our table and crossed him three times, too."

We were eating a delicious rye pie with berries, drinking hot, strong black tea with some fragrant herbs, and suddenly, out of nowhere, we started talking about politics. Although it all started with that amazing, unusual pie. It all started with the revelations of the Train Master, who happened to be nearby at an inopportune moment. The

Metropolitan saw him through a crack in the curtains and beckoned him to the table.

"Tell me, Maxim Fyodorovich, my dear man, please. We shout it to the whole world: a great people, language, culture, the largest country in the world by territory and natural resources. We have the most weapons of mass destruction. We are conquerors, we have defeated all the peoples around our Golden Ring, annexed them and given them the civilization of the Russian world, created a mighty, invincible empire in the world. Now no one is afraid of us; everyone is forced to reckon with us. Without our interests, there will be no peace on earth."

We don't need to prove anything anymore. All we need to do is detonate obsolete atomic and hydrogen bombs on our own soil, and the world will cease to exist. We're not Jews who've been cheating for millennia and sucking people's blood through all sorts of means: usury, lies, deceit, intrigue, and hypocrisy. We must say it straight out and point it out on the map: we are the Russian world—from here to here . Don't bother us anymore. If anything happens, it'll be the end for everyone. We need to bang on the UN podium like Khrushchev. And say it loudly: after us, even the deluge.

Everything is fine and wonderful, but there are a million problems. The main one is, no one likes us. They're afraid of us, of course, but at the same time, they hate us with all their hearts. Speak for yourself, hand on your heart, admit it. I give you the cross (he crossed himself three times). I promise to leave you alone at this job if you tell me honestly. - What's the matter?

- Why is your train so gloomy and run-down, like a godforsaken abode for unfortunate travelers? It reminds me of Mother Russia in some way. The compartments, toilets, vestibules, the restaurant, and the carriages themselves are terrible, and the smells everywhere are unpleasant. We haven't even been in a reserved seat carriage yet, and you probably still have general carriages. - Why don't you have food for passengers in the restaurant? It's all Chinese crap. - You don't have a doctor on the train, what if someone needs emergency help, and the station is still a long way away. We saw the first aid kit today. It only had tourniquets, cotton wool, bandages, paracetamol, iodine, and brilliant green. This is a mockery of people. - Aren't you ashamed to even bother making excuses? - You can't manage a team.

Well, now speak, I'm listening. Just please don't drag Aglaya Petrovna into this. We have plenty of Aglayas like you in Rus', but there aren't enough for everyone. As the saying goes, keep your mouth shut.

The train conductor, a man named Sutuly, was completely dejected, standing there like a guilty brat, at a loss for how to extricate himself. Then he gathered his courage and loudly asked permission to sit down and pour some vodka for a toast. The priest nodded, and Maxim Fyodorovich poured vodka from a decanter for everyone and himself first, then said:

"Allow me, Holy Father, to drink to your words about Palestine. We are ignorant people, living, as you said, in the grayness of everyday life, knowing nothing of the outside world." "Who is to blame for this, except the Palestinians themselves? They should have kept those bastard Jews out of the country. They should have met the refugee ships with arms in hand... Well, more on that later."

I want to express my respect to you. Don't think I'm expressing my admiration for your knowledge out of self-interest. I've never thought of anything like what you said, or what I've overheard. It's as if a lightbulb went on somewhere in my mind, and I began to perceive the world in different colors. Now I'm wondering - was I really living in darkness before? So, I drink to your words... (After drinking and snacking on a piece of aspic sliced on a plate, he continued).

- I'll be honest with you, and I don't understand a thing. First, about my train. I liked how you compared it to Russia. There are so many similarities. There are especially many crooks, you could easily stab someone in the back. Theft is everywhere here, and everywhere too.

Back in the USSR, and even under Yeltsin, there was some kind of order. My train was considered one of the best in terms of service. There were sleeping cars, soft cars with two-person compartments, and one car with improved service for VIPs.

Of course, the chefs in the restaurant prepared hot dishes, and professional barmaids and waiters worked as expected. Everything was clean and comfortable. Most importantly, the people—the passengers—were very cultured, or rather well-mannered. The relationships between passengers and the service staff were cordial. That's no longer the case; communication is limited to barking.

Something has broken in the country; the government has become separated from the people, as if we're speaking different languages. Theft and plunder have led to the destruction of such a vast, rich socialist country in the history of the world, the dream of many generations of ordinary, honest people. What kind of disaster has happened in this era, to the mind of civilization? Everyone suddenly became a thief. I remember we left on the same shift in the 2000s, before the Zionists carried out their terrorist attack in New York in September. One night, the carpets disappeared in three train cars, my uniform coat was stolen, and all the cooks' stainless steel utensils were stolen. Later, word got out that the same thing had happened everywhere.

The cooks and waiters have scattered in all directions. Now it's time for the self-taught, loudmouthed, and incompetent bunglers. They want to make a quick buck without breaking a sweat. That's why our restaurant has such a poor selection: cheap Chinese fast food, canned goods, crackers, over-salted mushrooms and cucumbers. "Why over-salted, you ask?" "So they don't spoil," you'll answer. This really infuriates and irritates me. These beautiful mushrooms and cucumbers are fit to be displayed at an exhibition. But they're inedible. People buy them, then go back and try to wash them. But it's unlikely to work. I once bought a liter of porcini mushrooms, washed them for half an hour, and it was all to no avail. The most a capricious passenger can hope for is for our chef to order the required dishes from outside at the nearest station, and only if time permits.

That's exactly how it is with people, with the common people. Everyone's over-salted. Beautiful on the outside, but bitter inside. Unadapted to reality, but capable of overcoming difficulties. And those in power get all their desires abroad. Naturally, for a big price. That's how we live. Everyone around us is to blame for everything, except us, the warm-hearted and great ones.

Regarding my sleeping cars, they were once uncoupled from our train and replaced with general cars for short-distance passengers, with seats. Then a rumor spread that some bigwig boss paid whoever needed to have them coupled to him. I'll put it this way, to summarize. We Russians need nothing more than unity as a single nation. We are incapable of living individually; we need a barracks, however uncomfortable, but one for all. We shouldn't live every man for himself, but exist shoulder to shoulder for all our kin. We used to be united by the building of communism. Everyone lived and aspired to something. We need to come up with a common idea, clear and understandable for everyone.

- Vladimir Magomedov, who had been sitting here deep in thought for a long time, said.

"I heard something similar at an exercise two days ago from a Vice Admiral. We were celebrating a successful torpedo test; I'm also one of the developers. He proposed a toast. 'To Crimea!' He says Crimea should be taken back from Ukraine. Nikita Khrushchev, it turns out, illegally handed over our land to the Ukrainians, which is legally wrong."

- The learned man tried to continue his thoughts, but the priest interrupted him.

- Come to me, my dear friend Volodya. We need Vladimirs and Vladimirovichs too. What a handsome man you are! Let me kiss you.

- What are you standing there for, God's servant, Slouchy? Shut your mouth and let's spill it all over everyone.

"We need to take Crimea back. This idea will stir up Mother Rus'. We'll all rise up, come to life. We'll shake off our gray hairs and show the world what a fine fellow our Vice Admiral is... Write me his name later, Volodya, don't forget. I'll light a candle for him and whisper to whoever needs to know to take note of this patriot." "Crimea is exactly what we need! The people's spirits will rise."

You can't even imagine this miracle of rebirth. We, like the Phoenix, will rise again, the whole nation. We will finally rise from our knees to our full, gigantic height and strike the UN podium with our fists, like a mythical hammer. Everyone will be silent, the enemies will be silent for a long time, the sycophants will return to kiss asses. To Crimea. Crimea will be ours. This is a wonderful toast, let's drink standing. Stand up, my dears, we should pour Aglaya Petrovna a drink too. What would you like to drink, my beauty? Speak up, my dear, don't be shy.

By this time, Vladimir had already uncorked the Hennessy cognac, filled a glass, and handed it to the suddenly embarrassed girl. Everyone drank a glass and then started on the appetizers.

Suddenly, everyone's appetites awoke simultaneously, especially the bishop. His face flushed from the intensity of his eating, and he constantly wiped his greasy hands, face, and beard with napkins. For about five minutes, everyone kept their heads down, absorbed in their food, and into the silence that hung, the conductor's uncertain, trembling voice rang out.

"Holy Father, I know my people. Crimea is a holiday with drinking, only for three days. And then, by inertia, for another month, Jewish and Armenian journalists will be driving viewers crazy on Central Television and on radio at every station. That's not enough for universal unity. The timeframe is short; we need to think more globally about how and with what to infect society, so that it's like diving headfirst into the abyss."

The priest took the decanter, poured himself some vodka, and drank it silently. Everyone followed him, and not yet understanding what was happening, they also drank.

- After thinking for a moment, the priest, who had been sour at first, suddenly came to life again, his eyes again lit up with a sparkle, and he, stealthily and boldly glancing around, declared in a quiet, low voice.

- Our Azerbaijanis are also whining about something, the Georgians are getting really angry and raising all sorts of rotten questions.

We'll help the Armenian adversaries with weapons and slip their Catholicos some blackmail to blackmail their corrupt politicians, even if they're sly, gentiles who sit on two chairs, sometimes for us, sometimes for Europe. But Karabakh is still in their hands because of us.

We'll kill two birds with one stone. And this should temporarily shut the mouths of the Azeris and their Turkish handlers.

"The Georgians need to be broken over the knee; they're a truly vile, disgusting people. They're chatterboxes. Wherever they sit, they brag incessantly, 'We're this, we're that.' If it weren't for us Russians, their trace in history would have long since disappeared. We simply need to deal with them, harshly. Recognize Abkhazia and South Ossetia as independent and sovereign states. Now that's some time for the Russians to celebrate. We need to open two military bases in Kazakhstan. Increase the troop contingent in Tajikistan. Those are just some more holidays. Open a new base in Syria, so the bloodsuckers' knees will tremble."

- The train conductor, having gained courage, also got going.

"Holy Father, we actually need to take Donbas back from Ukraine. Everyone should know these are our ancestral territories. Our grandfathers and fathers didn't shed blood in vain."

- Here the bishop suddenly started rolling the barrel at me, apparently seeing from the expression on my face my displeasure with what I had said.

"Abdurakhman, you seem sad." "You obviously have something to say, or are you having problems with such ambitious plans for the evolution of statehood in the Russian Federation? Perhaps you're against the globalization of the Russian world altogether?"

- After such an unambiguous threatening tone from the priest, monk Gregory approached the table as if to check if there was anything unnecessary to remove. But the metropolitan shook his head and gestured for him to go to bed.

I had to resort to the dastardly art of Third World diplomacy - expressing my concern about the problems that had arisen and the hope that the parties involved could always find a peaceful solution to the issue.

"Yakov Stepanovich! My dear, you hold such a high rank and a special position in the Orthodox world. You, and no one else, should be interested in peace with our fraternal Ukrainian people. They are also Christians, the closest people by blood."

Moreover, if you recall the speech by Russian Prime Minister Putin, he clearly articulated his position in response to a journalist in 1999 regarding the inviolability of the borders between Ukraine and the Russian Federation. He also recently responded to a journalist's question about Crimea at a forum in 2006, already as President of the Russian Federation. Crimea is part of the Ukrainian state.

All of us, fraternal republics, emerged from the USSR's overcoat. We all need to be friends and help each other. We share a common history that goes back centuries, and we were a united country for many decades. If everyone starts making such proposals, it will be very dangerous. Our peoples are hot-blooded and not very law-abiding, they have a knack for military affairs, and ethnic tensions could arise.

You've also wrongly brought up other republics. I'm an Uzbek originally from Kazakhstan. If you know history, we used to be one great Turan, a Turkic people spread across the continents of Eurasia and North Africa. As Muslims, journalists in all media outlets castigate us and accuse us of terrorism and the violation of women's rights, and God knows what else terrible. But Islam is a religion of peace and goodness. The Quran, as the final book of Holy Scripture, was given to all people on the planet, to all the descendants of our forefather Adam and our foremother Eve. For us, villainy is a mortal sin. The murder of one innocent person is tantamount to the murder of all humanity. And furthermore, we cannot force a person to accept our faith against their will. It is haram; hell is definitely promised for such a crime.

To cool down a bit, I propose a toast - to brotherhood between the descendants of our forefather Adam!

At this point, more to tease than to engage in quotational banter, the bishop recalled September 11, 2001, the explosion of apartment buildings in Moscow and the Caucasus, which reignited the war in Chechnya.

I had to politely remind him about the "Ryazan Sugar" incident, when residents of a building in Ryazan were able to discover the criminals and defuse the explosives by involving the local police, rather than corrupt FSB agents.

Well, and as if by the way , about the two world wars with the deaths of tens of millions of victims, all the participants were Christians, and the actions took place mainly between Christian powers.

The murder of millions of civilians in the Middle East, the destruction of the world's most ancient cities, containing priceless architectural monuments and artifacts, by such virtuous countries as the United States, Russia, Great Britain, France, Spain, and other NATO members, all Christian by faith. This is true terrorism—the blatantly planned murder of millions of Muslims. All under Israeli control. As a result, millions of refugees fled to Europe. Over time, this will also create problems in the relationships between these unfortunate poor people and the wealthy locals with different cultural traditions and outlooks.

The Metropolitan wanted to touch on the expansion of Arab conquerors and the Turkish Sultanate when they conquered the countries of Christian Europe. But I skillfully parried his blow, recalling what the fanatics and knights who participated in the many Crusades did in their religious pursuits.

Our get-together was beginning to take on the characteristics of a pointless, partisan debate between well-intoxicated people. Then, suddenly, Aglaya Petrovna, who had previously remained shyly silent, revealed herself in an unexpected way.

- Oh, you guys! In a word, you're like little children. All so smart and pompous, but you don't see anything important or fundamental in the big picture. As kids say when they're playing war in the yard: "Peace to the world, war to the war."

Whether it's Crimea or Donbass...

We need to take all of Ukraine. In its entirety.

To drink, you have to drink. What's the point of something running down your mustache and nothing going into your mouth? If you're going to have fun, let's have fun. If you sin, let's do it with all your heart, so you'll have something to repent for later.

Silence fell over the dining car. I could feel my heart pounding in my chest with genuine disagreement with such a horrific proposal. I was ready to say that only live-eating hyenas had such an opinion.

But no one would have heard me. Madness ensued. The Metropolitan was the most delighted. He stepped up from the table and, posturing and gesturing with his arms as if he wanted to dance the lezginka like the Chechens, exclaimed:

- My dear Aglaya Petrovna Butusova! Let me kiss you, my dear woman... You look like a fish in the water... People like you should be carried in our arms and bathed in fresh milk three times a week. You are a beauty beyond compare. By this night I will forgive you all your sins, past and present.

What wise words and from whose lips? Women! Mothers!

Aglaya Petrovna, you are my homeland, I will elevate you to the palace today...

I should have said that, those thoughts were wandering around in my mind. - How could I have missed it and not thought of it... What wild, inviting eyes you have... Oh, I...

The Metropolitan ordered everyone to pour a full glass of vodka, except for the Train Master, who was ordered to go and personally inspect the detained suspects and the conductors' performance, then return and report on the overall situation. He also issued an official reminder.

"Maxim Fyodorovich, in half an hour you'll be giving a toast in my honor. The first, as befits every leader in the territory entrusted to the state. The congratulations will begin soon, be sure not to be late. Don't forget that friendship is friendship, but tobacco is apart. Don't even think about being late, my dear."

CHAPTER 19

The concepts offer possible scenarios for the development of various versions of taste trends in various directions of sensory associations, no matter what this concerns or affects in the creative pursuit of human exploration.

Allah the Almighty breathed life into our forefather Adam and thereby transmitted microparticles of potential in hereditary creativity, which was undoubtedly passed on in the form of a knowledge bank to generations of people.

Now this has become a subject of bargaining between religions, peoples, and ethnic groups. But no one speaks of forgery, lies, slander, the propaganda of falsehoods, or disinformation. It's probably no secret that moneylenders (banks) have always accepted the most valuable collateral for loans: knowledge, books, discoveries... Scientists have always been largely artlessly careless and never valued their time, perhaps because of this they have always remained in need of material means of subsistence, that is, defenseless. Moneylenders have always found ways to apply and utilize this intellectual research and knowledge to their own material benefit.

There's a concept that has always remained contemporary in any era of change, one that Zionist psychoanalytic fanatics tried to banish from the human subconscious. The meaning of God, parents, family, and surnames, among those they considered goyim. Cattle.

What is almost impossible to prove becomes difficult to disprove. Since the time of the prophet Moses, everything has remained as before.

Sodom and Gomorrah. The Golden Calf. The tribes of Israel returned to the Holy Land of Canaan for the second time, not with good intentions, as warm-hearted refugees seeking refuge with honey and olive branches, but as fierce hyenas, sinners scenting blood, with sword and fire.

The most beautiful woman in the world and the most important woman to me is my mother. The strongest, fairest, most courageous, wisest, and best friend is my father. Anyone who thinks differently is entitled to their own opinion.

Some people have nothing to be proud of in this regard, and they begin to be disingenuous in their reasoning and look for maneuvers to fill the void with exotic ideas.

"But the most beautiful and best in the world are our women. We have such a fearless spirit and unwavering willpower and courage. Wow, don't you dare go against it. Our scientists, warriors, athletes, and those in power see no obstacles in their path. They're ready to claim not only forests and fields, but also the North and South Poles, and even plots of land on the Moon, Mars, and the vastness of space."

Prophets are understood by absolutely everyone; their words are clear and intelligible to all. This phenomenon cannot be cultivated in any way, for it is a gift from God. Priests, clergy, and other supposed authorities in the spiritual hierarchy cannot achieve this, for they have fallen out of the human fold.

All specializations in the study of the human psyche cannot even come close to conceptually qualifying as a scientific discipline, as each human being is unique and unrepeatable. Concepts such as clinical psychology, social psychology, neuropsychology, developmental psychology, educational psychology, family psychology, coaching, art therapy, psychotherapy, and all related fields in philosophy, sociology, biology, and economics cannot provide the coordinates and reference points for compiling a theoretical and methodological database. The study of the human psyche is a complete terra incognita. Therefore, psychoanalysis should under no circumstances be used in the education system, in marriage, or in legal proceedings. The concept of sane/insane should be determined only at the scene of the incident in the presence of more than three witnesses, with the possibility of a re-examination with other participants in the procedure after at least two days. This would be correct.

Places for holding prisoners serving long sentences, prisons, and psychiatric hospitals are all subject to abolition. All legal proceedings must be conducted in accordance with Sharia law, in the name of Almighty God. Conduct an independent referendum among lawyers, after first studying the fundamental principles of all existing courts. Sharia law will benefit everyone, in every way.

The calls began—or rather, there were only two—with congratulatory messages. The first was from the Metropolitan Bishop, head of the Russian Orthodox Church in Vladivostok. They spoke briefly, only pleasantries, and simultaneously, interrupting each other. The second call was from relatives, probably a mother, aunt, or sister, but certainly not a wife. The phone was on speakerphone, and the voice was that of an old man, feeble and painfully coughing. The priest addressed the caller with a respectful, loving "Vy." It was clear the Metropolitan was nervous and waiting for the calls. He frequently glanced at his sparkling diamond-studded Rolex watch.

Vladimir and I were discussing an interesting issue about poverty. How, in times of need, people are capable of all sorts of illegal and immoral acts that they would never commit if they had the relative material security of a comfortable life.

That not only the fear of God, but also this awareness of the presence of good would keep him from the risk of losing everything because of suddenly emerging self-interest.

I only managed to formulate the thought that in Islam, poverty is not a problem, ignorance is a vice.

In their search for an understanding of God and the divine attributes, many people tend to fall into blasphemy out of ignorance, that is, ignorance. This is probably why many new converts to the understanding of Monotheism are harsh in their judgments and intolerant in their opinions, and often in their actions.

- A slightly thoughtful archbishop approached us and spoke as if reluctantly.

"God's servant Alexander Litvinenko presented himself to God's judgment today. Although you wouldn't wish such a death on your worst enemy." "How long did the fool suffer?" "The main reason he endured all this torture?" "What's the point? So, figure out where the truth lies." This story is so confusing, you can't immediately understand the meaning of existence, the real reasons for the conflict of interests. "Who's telling the truth, who's lying, who's the murderer? We only know who died."

I heard you talking about material values.

"What's the point of wealth if you lack the conscience and brains to properly utilize it? That's what we need to think about..."

Some naive people think it would be great to win millions of dollars in the lottery. But they don't realize how many risks they immediately face. Few are prepared to manage such luck wisely. Family and friends also face various trials. And we haven't even mentioned malicious intent, envy, or jealousy. And then there are the evildoers who might try...

- Vladimir asked during the momentary pause, more out of politeness than interest.

"Yakov Stepanovich, while you're waiting for calls from important people, perhaps you could tell me something about this Alexander Litvinenko. You mentioned him with such warmth in your voice, as if you knew him personally in the past."

The priest quickly turned around, crossed himself three times, and answered.

"God bless you, Vladimir. Of course you didn't know. If you had, maybe his life would have turned out differently. I heard a lot about this story. I remember his speech with his colleagues at a press conference, when they announced that the heads of the 7th Department of the Directorate for the Development and Suppression of Criminal Organizations and the Federal Security Service of the Russian Federation had given them illegal orders to kill Boris Berezovsky and some Chechen businessman, as well as some FSB officer."

I remember Litvinenko personally meeting with Vladimir Vladimirovich Putin; he'd just become Director of the FSB. Something didn't seem to click between them. They knew each other well, and not just from their work. It's not a good thing. Then the sinner started writing libels about his comrade, claiming he was a pedophile, that he was the head of an organized crime group, and that he had created a syndicate system to control drug trafficking and illegal prostitution practically worldwide. Just think about it. Such things are not forgiven.

At that moment, the train conductor, Maxim Fyodorovich Sutuly, literally came running. He immediately ordered the girl Aglaya to bring a kettle of warm water and a basin so the Metropolitan and his guests could wash their hands. The priest clearly liked the offer and smiled. When he finished washing his hands, he even sprinkled some drops on the girl's face with his fingertips, flirtatiously.

Before sitting down at the table, the archbishop once again inquired about the time, then, shaking his head, said:

--Something is wrong in our kingdom. The Tsar Father, through the lips of his assistants, has not pleased us insignificant mortals with a heartfelt congratulation.

The Most Holy Lord knows everything there is to know about us good fellows and where we, God's servants, are from reports... And he did not deign to do so. His Holiness the Patriarch of Moscow and All Rus' knows how to convey necessary information through his silence.

The brothers of the Synod have not expressed their wishes for many years. As has always been the case in the past two years, I was elevated to rank for my service and labors.

Well, good health and well-being to everyone! Sit down and enjoy your meal. Here, our beautiful Aglaya has heated up some buckwheat porridge and some cutlets. Eat up, Abdurakhman, don't worry, it's all beef. I don't like pork either; even lard is too heavy for me.

Well, my dear friend, Train Master, you have the floor. Just don't get too overzealous with the green snake, Maxim Fyodorovich; you're on duty, after all. Watch out who catches the scent, and you'll be in trouble later, even without my criticism. Be stern and specific.

"Citizen Sutuly, although he was the Train Master, turned out to have no gift for eloquence and no sense of humor. His attempts at humor nearly resulted in a minor conflict over his offensive remarks directed at various mentally deficient black people and people of Caucasian descent. These people, he claimed, were supposedly naturally prone to terrorism due to their low ethnocultural standards, stemming from racial, religious, and ethnic intolerance..."

Of course, I immediately expressed my protest delicately, only out of respect for the birthday boy, calling the boss a Nazi, blindly falling into the arms of fascism due to ignorance.

But how furious and enraged our quiet and balanced physicist turned out to be in his anger; he almost flipped the table when he tried to reach across it to turn the offender around and look him in the eyes.

"I've been a Corresponding Member of the Russian Academy of Sciences for several years, almost an Academician. What are you even thinking, you bastard, you fascist mug? I'm a pure Avar from the Caucasus, I have two medals, you bastard... Your brain is as tiny as a chicken from an incubator, you're a lost specimen for society. A fucking parasite."

- The Metropolitan sharply raised his hand and placed it on the shoulder of the Train Master and said in a surprisingly calm, even voice.

" Do you remember that Soviet film about the little black boy whom Russian sailors from the corvette Bogatyr picked up from a storm-battered American ship and raised as a cabin boy? Well, that African-American boy was named Maximka. So, he's your namesake. I remember at the end of the film, the captain of the Russian corvette assigned the boy to the crew as a cabin boy and gave him the last name Bogatyrev."

So go and think about your words, former train conductor Maximka.

Stooped Maxim Fedorovich dropped only a few words and left us.

"Father, you yourself asked us to tell only the truth. Our people think the same way. All Russians hate them and only endure it through gritted teeth. All our problems are because of them."

- Following him, the Metropolitan spoke.

"No matter how much of a half-wit he is, he's still telling a terrible secret. We know what people confess to us. Everyday life has eaten away at people's feelings, their lack of well-being."

The majority of the population, in the twenty-five years since the collapse of the USSR, has suddenly and rapidly descended into a state of stupefaction. People have suddenly lost the ability to act rationally, analytically, and logically.

So many swindlers, fraudsters, scoundrels, and money-grubbers have sprung up. I won't even mention the hundreds of thousands of parasites and drones that have appeared. They're sucking the good energy and strong blood out of our mother Russia, and our thickheads, like that idiot Maximka, blame it all on people from their sister republics.

Nazi devils like him should be hanged, but not on the Honor Roll, of course.

CHAPTER 20

The priest tried to read the poems like rap, rhythmically shaking his head.

I grew up in the urban taiga, a graveyard of dark streets. I learned my lessons amidst swamps of all sorts of trials, amid mountains of egoism and arrogance, amid seas of flowing tears, amidst a tundra of despair... I ate my share of salt, tasted sorrow, and experienced grief for my weaknesses, amidst an ocean of empty emotions of the parched Soviet era.

Aglaya hovered around the Metropolitan, and they whispered jokes and smiled. The TV series "Comedy Club" was playing endlessly.

Vladimir and I sat next to each other, eating buckwheat porridge and roasted wild goose, discussing when the tensions between Ukraine and Russia began. We identified the active phase of the mutual grievances as the 2004 presidential election. What was most surprising was the Kremlin's incomprehensible obstinacy?! We recalled the events of recent years, especially since they were a novelty in the vastness of the USSR, as all former citizens of that once-great country clearly saw how conspiracy theories work.

At that time, the Kremlin wanted to see its candidate, Viktor Yanukovych, as president, while the West wanted a loyal candidate to win, appealing to the concepts of the democratic development of the country and attempting to master European thinking while fulfilling the duties of the President of Ukraine, Viktor Yushchenko.

Two rounds of presidential elections were held. Following scandals involving alleged interference in the elections, a rerun was scheduled for December 26, 2004, which was won by Viktor Yushchenko.

Of course, his victory was largely miraculous, due to the fact that Yushchenko was attacked by unknown forces, injected with a dose of dioxin during a dinner with a high-ranking Ukrainian intelligence official. The candidate's face was disfigured by abscesses and tumors, his physical condition was undermined, and he was unable to speak at rallies. The recovery process will likely be lifelong, as it is very difficult to completely eliminate the dioxin.

Be that as it may, victory was hard-won due to popular unrest, which was heightened by the many secret spells cast by the supernatural spirits, the brownies, who joined in the people's prayers. Viktor Yanukovych's supporters had unlimited resources to rig the election results in his favor, but they mysteriously and incomprehensibly yielded.

Perhaps the freedom-hungry people were unwilling to accept such total, unlawful interference in the election process. Ultimately, the Supreme Court of Ukraine declared the election results inconsistent with the will of the voters and ordered a rerun.

Relations between Moscow and Kiev are now clearly strained, even hostile, the kind often found in married couples on the eve of an imminent divorce, when partners are fed up with each other and tired of it. The enticing scent of freedom is deceptive, amidst the lofty hopes of one partner, yearning to escape a stifling, stale atmosphere. The other is experiencing a storm of emotions, racked by the torment of losing control over a previously subordinate family member, the loss of perceived authority in the relationship, and the supposed naivety of their minds. And, of course, the acute pain of emotional anguish. There's jealousy over a neglected body—now easily accessible to all sorts of amorous sex seekers with perversions—with its mind-bending charms. But this is, undoubtedly, a delusion.

This feeling is akin to the initial state of intoxication, depending on the subject's mood. A good, uplifting mood produces one result, while anger and jealousy produce another. Decisions should be made rationally, first separating from the spouse for a while and returning to blood relatives to recharge with the lost energy of the family. Then, having calmed down, bringing one's feelings to a state of dispassion, so that the mind is freed from doubts and mirages, one should begin to investigate the causes of conflicts, analyze events, and reach a verdict. The clarity of the decision's penetration into the mind and ecology of the thinking individual must be consistent with the paradigm that the decision was right for all sides of the family. Otherwise, the trail left behind by this couple will be trodden upon not only by those with the intent but also by malicious enemies.

The Kremlin, while harboring a grudge, nonetheless actively supports Yanukovych's party with massive cash injections to bolster its candidate's ratings, despite his appearance, moral character, and two criminal convictions. 1. In 1968, he was sentenced for complicity in gang rape. He served a three-year sentence in Penal Colony No. 14 in Mariupol. 2. In 1978, he was sentenced for hooliganism (racketeering) causing moderate bodily harm. He served a three-year sentence in Penal Colony No. 121 in the village of Stepnoye in the Donetsk region.

So think about it after that. It's strange. - Couldn't they have found anyone better out of the millions?

The vodka was doing its dirty work, despite the fact that we were snacking on fatty foods, drinking water, and all sorts of tasty drinks. We didn't notice where the priest and his girlfriend, Aglaya, had disappeared to. We talked about the problems of Russia, the fraternal republics of the former USSR, the former socialist republics, and the supposedly free, once-Christian, militant West, now completely occupied by a secret underground sect of a powerful Zionist mafia clan.

How much misery has the imperial ambitions of vanished mighty empires, possessing vast territories and countless advantages for metropolitan residents over provinces, protectorates, and colonies, caused to peoples? Any perceived superiority is a mirage, a veil of decay, a veil of darkness, inevitably ending in tragedy for future generations. Not to mention race, ethnicity, religion, and other signs of intolerance.

Now, once again, the Colossi with feet of clay are visible in the foreground. Problems with anticipated military conflicts have surfaced, as usually happens when Jews begin to live in prosperity. Immediately, their misunderstanding of God's chosenness clouds their minds and drives them crazy.

And let's not forget the myths of "Russian greatness," the Celestial Empire, the treacherous Foggy Albion, and America's claim to be the Third Rome. Humanity cannot avoid trouble. Amid such intrigues, with the Prevost of some countries over the Right of another, a majority of poor and wretched countries, disaster is certain. Conflicts in understanding the world order are inevitable, and hence conflicts, wars, and murders.

It's high time to rid ourselves of these base addictions. To save life on earth, we must return to a life in accordance with God's Laws, where everyone has equal rights and equal responsibilities. Above all, we must restore freedom of speech in all media and pass a law criminalizing the open propaganda of lies, the dissemination of false information, and deliberate disinformation. Ban the use of the term "psychoanalysis" in the education system, in the courts, and in all spheres of human interaction. Stop the social programming of NLP societies with mind-control practices involving the greatness of nations, languages, cultures, and God's chosenness. Particularly condemn thinking in social groups and larger communities in terms of hateful theories: imperialism, fascism, Zionism, Marxism, and atheism. The subcultural, defective ornamentalism of these theories can be understood through personal, optional study.

The Law of God is just in every respect, with impeccable wisdom. The words of the Most High Lord are absolute truth and can convey nothing if they do not correspond perfectly. Anything that can be found that is biased or at odds with the truth is the fruit of human intervention. There is much in the Torah (Torah), Psalms (Zabur), and the Gospel (Injeel) that is blatantly abhorrent and does not correspond to truth, reality, or justice. Yet, all the flaws and shortcomings in the Scriptures are clearly and concisely edited by the Quran. The Law of Allah, the Lord of the worlds, immediately acquires a harmony of meaning, sublime beauty, and the absolute wisdom of the Most High Creator of space and time.

- What is this that Jews have been appealing to for millennia? Is this what the goyim will love them for?

(Deuteronomy, Chapter 23, /especially 1,2,3, 7/ text 19.20)

19 - You shall not lend to your brother on interest, either silver or grain or anything else that can be lent on interest.

20 – You shall lend to a foreigner on interest, but you shall not lend to your brother on interest, so that the Lord your God may bless you in everything you put your hand to in the land where you go to possess it.

This is clearly an addendum; the author is undoubtedly a cunning, selfish, hunchbacked money lender.

The Torah contains so much horror, approving of the mass murder of peoples encountered by the Jews, who were executed without any guilt. How much violence they inflicted on thousands of people, simply for the fun of it, or for what purpose, is unclear. And this is the religion of one special people, closed off from all other bestial ones.

The Holy Scriptures are all from the Most High God, and therefore should, in theory, be the ultimate truth, flawlessly accurate and completely fair.

The Torah is supposedly written by the prophet Moses, but at the same time, there's a scene where he writes about himself while buried in an unknown location. What is this? How is that possible? It's absolutely impossible. (Deuteronomy 34)

1. And Moses went up from the plains of Moab to Mount Nebo, to the top of Pisgah, which is over against Jericho: and the Lord showed him all the land of Gilead, as far as Dan,

2. and all... Naphtali, and ... the land of Ephraim and Manasseh, and all the land of Judah, even to the western sea,

3. and the south country, and the plain of the valley of Jericho, the city of palm trees, as far as Zoar.

4. And the Lord said to him, "This is the land which I sware to Abraham, Isaac, and Jacob, saying, 'To your seed I will give it.' I have shown you the land, but you shall not enter it."

5. And Moses the servant of the Lord died there in the land of Moab, according to the word of the Lord,

6. And he was buried in the valley of the land of Moab, opposite Beth-peor; and no man knoweth... his burial unto this day.

7. Moses was one hundred and twenty years old when he died, but his sight was not dimmed, and his strength was not weakened.

This can't be true. Not at all. In no way. Someone else wrote it. And there's plenty of this and other texts that are downright repugnant to the sober mind. And the Gospels contain precisely the same problems. That's why they're all named after this and that. The reader is deliberately informed beforehand: "Errors, inaccuracies, information from third parties, and allegories are possible, depending on the narrator's intellect." This in no way excuses the scribes' creative potential. Therefore, Holy Scripture is very easy to understand after studying the Quran; all texts become accessible and understandable in all their beautiful harmony and justice.

The Torah contains many contradictions, errors, flaws, shortcomings, horrific scenes of murder and perjury by the Jewish people, all of which are clearly encouraged and justified by the Almighty God. This cannot be, for the Almighty is generous, wise, and just.

The Messiah Jesus/Yeshua/Christ (the prophet Isa) was sent to the Jewish people, specifically to those who had strayed from the straight path of monotheism. He states this directly, saying that he came not to abolish God's law, but to return sinners to it. Another point that can be found in the Gospel text is: At the dawn of Zionism in Europe, they wrote:

A clear sign (of the coming of the Antichrist) is the prosperity of the Jews, who are increasing in number and gathering everywhere, enjoying such great privileges that we should seriously fear the Lord's wrath, lest He allow the Antichrist to come. For you see how the clergy and faithful Christians daily suffer oppression and the curtailment of their rights and liberties, and endure many insults. The synagogue prospers more than the Church of Christ, and among princes, any Jew can achieve more than a nobleman or prelate. Indeed, princes and barons are ruined by unheard-of interest rates, as if (the Jews) could use these treasures to enrich and support their master, the Antichrist.

This section is notorious for containing one of the first systematic theories of "blood accusation." (Anti-Semitic) Judeophobic content.

In this passage, Thomas claims that because of the Jews' supposed role in Christ's crucifixion, they suffered from a bleeding disease. To cure it, he suggests they deliberately killed Christians and used their blood in rituals.

Whenever you're looking for someone to blame, especially in terrorist attacks allegedly committed by stupid Muslims, I ask you to remember the old Jewish lawyer who, in his time, served in various roles in legal proceedings (judge, prosecutor, defense attorney, expert witness, juror, victim, witness, always and in everything accused of self-interest and treachery, but never accused of a crime). He only revealed an open secret in a state of unconsciousness before his death, confessing frankly in his delirium... – Whenever I tried criminal and civil cases against bloodthirsty moneylenders, even in my robes, I always tried to pierce the minds of the jurors and spectators with one concept: WHO BENEFIT FROM THIS?

Hence the conclusion. Zionism and fascism are essentially twin murderers. Moreover, Zionism is far more terrifying, for it kills with the hands and means of others involved in the propaganda of lies and poisonous disinformation. Zionism is the father of corruption.

Corruption and usury provided an opportunity to influence public opinion. Napoleon was apparently right in his expert assessment of a statesmanlike ruler.

The Jewish nation's activities since the time of Moses, by virtue of its entire predisposition, have consisted of usury and extortion. It is a nation within a nation... Entire villages have been robbed by the Jews, they have reintroduced slavery; they are veritable flocks of ravens.

At one station, we wanted to get out for some fresh air, but it was pitch dark and impossible to see. Somewhere in the distance, a lonely lightbulb glowed, illuminating part of the wall of a one-story brown building and a blue door. We didn't dare try to get out for a walk, especially since there was no conductor in the vestibule. Just as Vladimir lit a cigarette, a priest appeared, smiling apologetically.

"My friends, I am a sinner, as are all people in the world, because of the mortal sin of our forefather Adam and our foremother Eve. Only through his cruel death on the cross did the Son of God, Jesus Christ, atone for all our sins, including mine. I am a sinner, a sinner, I repent." (He crossed himself three times.)

That's it, Adamovich, put out your teat, I can't breathe. Let's go have fifty grams each. Otherwise, I'm going to feel sick.

We obediently followed the Metropolitan. It turned out the decanter was empty, and no one dared go to the compartment where, according to the priest, Aglaya had slept naked. Vladimir poured everyone cognac and proposed a toast to world peace. Everyone drank it without hesitation, as it turned out, a very tasty drink after the vodka.

The priest was quite drunk, although he managed to hide it, but from time to time his symptoms were noticeable.

"My masculine strength seems to have deserted me in this turmoil. Perhaps the Lord has spared me from yet another demonic temptation? Aglaya, with her cunning, lured me into her net; I don't understand how I ended up in her hot embrace with these large goods . Fortunately, my penis didn't respond, not even to her ardent efforts with kisses. The damned Satan leads everyone into fornication."

I've heard your conversations... You all seem to speak with balance and meaning, it seems, but a lot, but in your reasoning. You don't have complete information, and therefore your analyses are fragmented. You can't draw a complete picture based on one episode. - Where do you get the links of the chains and assemble the information into a single necklace? - Of course, the internet, TV and radio news, well, newspapers of all kinds, most of it is public opinion. Family and friends have said something, friends and acquaintances have shared their knowledge, others have told you things by chance.

If you develop your business like this, bankruptcy is just around the corner. The axe is always there, and the stump is not far away. We, too, used to work tirelessly, never sleeping, trying to figure out how the Jews were using their accumulated financial skills. Although, in principle, we still lag behind all the churches in the proper management and use of funds, movable and immovable property, luxury goods, and antiques. The Soviet Union was plundered in the 1990s by the Jews, who knew no fear, and they are tired of it. They are also the thieves in the governments of the USSR and the Russian Federation, and especially active party and parliamentary leaders, among them, have succeeded everywhere. Well, judge for yourself.

In 1991, the UN General Assembly adopted an immoral, unprecedented decision to repeal the 1975 resolution. So what kind of resolution was that? So, experts, answer? That's the point: you can't, because you don't know. Fine. I'll help you. In 1975, the Arab countries, suffering colossal hardships—all sorts of problems artificially created by the US and European NATO member states, naturally (for the sake of security interests and Israel's enrichment) under the leadership of Zionists entrenched in governments and parliaments—came forward with an initiative to adopt a resolution condemning Zionism as a form of racism and racial discrimination at the 30th session of the UN General Assembly.

During the discussion, international Zionism was condemned by the socialist countries, particularly for the expansion of the aggressive state of Israel, which kills people around the world without trial or investigation, harboring and failing to extradite international criminals, murderers, and corrupt officials who escaped with stolen millions, as well as thousands of victims of swindlers and fraudsters, led by corrupt Zionists. This resembles the spread of a cancerous tumor in the body of humanity. Incidentally, I'm quoting speeches from representatives of socialist countries, especially the USSR. Our KGB was head and shoulders above all other intelligence agencies in the world, including the US, UK, and especially Israel. A film called "Secret and Overt" was made several years before 1975.

No one could get away with it; all the facts were there. Moreover, they carried out detailed coverage of the events in Hungary, Poland, and the Prague Spring, identifying everywhere the planners, organizers, and active participants in the subversion of communist parties in Europe. And it was all orchestrated by Zionists. Wherever there's something illegal to profit from, they're always there, ready to carry out operations.

UN General Assembly Resolution 3379, "The Elimination of All Forms of Racial Discrimination," was adopted on November 10, 1975, at the 30th session of the UN General Assembly. It classified Israel as a state practicing apartheid and declared Zionism a form of racism and racial discrimination, as well as a threat to international peace and security.

"We literally sat there with our mouths open. We'd never heard anything like it before." The priest, seeing our surprise, continued.

-- After all, the USSR initially advocated a solution to the Jewish question, integrating it into the doctrine and concept of world revolution within the Marxist-Leninist project. This adaptation failed because the Zionists, entrenched at the pinnacle of power in the Soviet Union, had entirely different goals. They sabotaged the execution of the Politburo's orders with minor adjustments, resulting in a completely different outcome. For example, the outcome of the Six-Day War in 1967 was completely emblematic in every sense: it was a victory for Zionists in all countries, including the USSR and the socialist countries. The supposed enemies of the world community, the US and the USSR, somehow defeated (through the combined efforts of Zionists in their governments) the Arab forces.

After all, even the incorruptible, ascetic leader of the world revolution was once duped by Zionists in the Politburo and the Central Committee of the CPSU, the NKVD and KGB, the Supreme Soviet, and the Ministry of Foreign Affairs. Jews were everywhere, and under their influence, the USSR was the first to recognize the State of Israel. Then, in 1953, having collected all the information about the Judeo-Mason affair, Stalin attempted to conduct a large-scale audit of government agencies to identify deeply entrenched Zionist agents, but they got ahead of him, managing to poison him with an unknown poison.

- Come on, Vladimir, pour some more cognac into the container, it goes well with hunting sausages.

I have a toast to my parents. My mother has grown old, completely lost her strength after my father's death. May he rest in peace (the Metropolitan stood and crossed himself three times). Let us drink, friends, to our parents, and to us, too. I have three sons, all in the military. Warriors.

I'm very worried about Moscow and Kyiv. We have one faith, one church. We mustn't destroy the unity of Orthodoxy. After all, we began with Kievan Rus'. It wasn't we, the Moscow Principality, but they, the Kievan Principality, who adopted the Christian faith first. We mustn't divide the church in any way; schism will destroy it.

We drank and snacked on smoked hunter's sausages. The interesting thing was that they were made in Iran. At least that's what the package said. They were very tasty, with a tart aroma, but a little hard. The Metropolitan called over the sullen, overweight cook, who, having woken up at 4 a.m., had been sorting through various bags in the kitchen with her assistant, preparing to greet the passengers for breakfast. Despite her plumpness, the woman arrived very quickly. "Please make us some tea. There should be a tin of loose-leaf Ceylon tea on the table. Make it strong. Thank you in advance, and may God bless you."

The priest crossed the woman three times, then motioned for Vladimir to fill the glasses. After everything had been poured, the Metropolitan cut a ripe pear into three pieces and, handing each of us a piece, offered us a toast to all the children in the world, especially to our own.

- It was obvious that the archbishop was really drunk, his voice changed and his speech became a little slurred, his tone changed and became harsher in his definitions.

"If we're going to take Crimea or start with Kyiv, we'll have to be incredibly subtle." "Do we have any brains in the Ministry of Defense? I don't know. Not everyone measures things in money."

Only with knives, arrows, and spears should we work silently to force the Nazi-Ukies to surrender and take captive. We must work bloodlessly, so the media doesn't see the bloodshed. Send three thousand death row inmates to major cities as businessmen, construction workers, laborers, drivers, and prostitutes. And then, all at once, carry out a silent operation and immediately install acting officers in key positions everywhere, so that life goes on as if nothing happened. Show good programs about friendship on TV and radio, organize all sorts of concerts throughout Ukraine with lotteries. Organize fairs with pancakes and caviar giveaways in cities and villages, and maybe we'll somehow get through the swamp of passions. We need to build a new fence and separate ourselves from Europe; we have no common ground with assholes and lesbians.

Zionists never sleep, always preparing poisons, sharpening knives, and counting the money in other people's pockets. Therefore, it is easy for them to kill, rape, pillage, betray, cheat, be mean, lie, grovel, and create problems for the sake of personal and Jewish gain. They have no self-criticism and have never had a guilty conscience. Their morality is elastic, for they despise all other goyim and do not consider them equals.

Well, what is this? Listen. This is Deuteronomy 15:6, the fifth book of Moses.

For the Lord your God will bless you, as he promised you, and you will lend to many nations, but you will not borrow; and you will rule over many nations, but they will not rule over you .

The Freemasons, like the Jewish moneylenders, have always sought and attempted to fan the flames between Christians and Muslims in order to reap enormous material and spiritual profits from this conflict. War always means violence, destruction, pain, and death, with rivers of blood flowing freely. Well, what's there to hide? Consider the terrible battles and conflicts throughout history, wherever they occurred. Conquests in the name of religion, colonialism, or political and economic reasons.

Wars between Christian countries in World Wars I and II claimed tens of millions of lives, specifically Christians. So, who killed whom? Christians killed Christians. It's like St. Bartholomew's Day massacre, only on a grander scale.

Wars where Christians, for one reason or another, launched collective operations against Muslims were always provoked by the Jews. They resulted in the murder of millions of lives, specifically those of meek yet courageous Muslims. Their faith simply amazes me with its strength of conviction; they believe with their hearts and minds. Now think about what this means. Whether you like it or not, you have to admit it. The Christian religion is the murder of civilians at the request, the plan, or the provocation of the Zionists.

- Okay, heads up, perk up. Here's the tea. Hot. There was some dark chocolate here somewhere, a bar. Break off a piece with some cognac. My toast.

We are the nomadic Horde. Golden. White. Blue. From East to West. We are the Turks, conquerors of the world of the ignorant, the enlightened, and the savages. We are the Hyperborean Varangians, masters of the seas, forests, fields, and mountains. We must be victors everywhere. We are the chosen ones, the Great People. The Russian world is the dream of the titans of thought. Those who said, "Whoever is not with us is against us," are right.

Those who are with us must bow their heads and accept the inevitable, live for the triumph of our ideals, or perish in the struggle. These days, we can't just smoke the skies. Everyone will have to choose a side and take a stand. We don't need the Hitler Youth, and we won't tolerate the cunning, blood-sucking parasites of the Zionists, but we won't give up our lion's share of politics and economics to anyone. We'll divide the world into our zones of interest, and then the next stage will be just two seats left for the competition—the third one is superfluous. - So, shall we drink to our shared victory?

In a war between believers and non-believers, the believers must always win. That's the law. But still, my soul is uneasy. We are led by a lieutenant colonel with the mind of a warrant officer.

"We drank without clinking glasses, as is customary at Russian funerals. Our priest suggested it, and he immediately began explaining why Muslims should stand with the Orthodox against the dull-witted Catholics, who are ruled by Protestants and Zionists."

Then the Metropolitan explained at length why in the satirical weekly Charle Hebdo in Paris is deliberately being staged by Jews attacking Islam. They maintain a certain temperature in the madhouse, raising and lowering the level of tension in public opinion. They keep their tentacles on the pulse so that a certain temperature always obediently fluctuates when they need it.

"Vladimir and I soon realized the priest was in a state of anxiety when a disturbingly copious drooling discharge began to appear from his mouth. He constantly wiped his mouth with napkins and shuddered several times, causing Vladimir to quickly move away from him. But the Metropolitan was carried away, lost somewhere in the distance, toward mirages."

"The Arabs managed to exploit their natural resources in a short period of time." "What's wrong with us?" "Why have thieves infiltrated all our governments? Because Stalin is gone."

I recently visited a sheikh from the Emirates and couldn't get him to understand what they need to do to improve the literacy of their population. I told him to open bookstores everywhere, book houses like libraries, teach your people not only to rejoice and pray, but also to be educated. The internet and computers are great, but we also need to use our brains to teach children. So, I explained to him, we need to make sure that the "Around the Corner" store always exists in the country. The world is always a correlation between Manhattan and Brooklyn. If you're on the rise in business, you strive to be closer to the Empire State Building, Times Square, Broadway. But if you're having financial problems, you'll have to move to Brooklyn...

He shakes his head and shrugs. He just doesn't get it. The scariest part of this story isn't online dating, but falling in love with your typewriter.

In short, no matter how hard he tried, he didn't understand me. - Maybe the translator didn't translate it correctly?

He was also saying something to me, trying to pull the wool over my eyes. He upset me so much with his incomprehensible associations to life's questions that I just blurted it out... I suggested he make a film with Meg. Ryan in a hijab. He liked the idea immediately. He says he liked the actress, especially in roles opposite Tom Hanks. A minute later, he understood the bookstore story. That's how it happens.

I've been to the UAE twice and liked a lot. I even envied them that we, with such opportunities, don't even come close to such abundance in any comparative sense. They have different people. Ours would steal or simply ruin everything. The culture is different.

The Metropolitan poured the remaining cognac into shot glasses, trying to give everyone an equal share. He did it so quickly that he exclaimed, "A master's craft fears a master's craft." Then he proposed a toast to the strength of the Muslim faith. He explained that in Moscow, for three million Muslims, there are only four mosques, while for two hundred thousand Jews, the state has authorized the construction of six large synagogues and about fifty prayer houses, and an unknown number of community centers, all built at state expense.

"I just don't understand how these Muslims love to pray and praise Allah Almighty so much, considering they're the dispossessed and suffer from our actions, too. It's us, not them, who are putting obstacles in their way... God forbid if they all rise up against these constant, absurd accusations from Israel and NATO military attacks.

No one will get off easy. Of course, we and the Chinese will support them. As they say, the enemy of our enemy is our friend..."

If we were to take every single Muslim and kill them all at once, for example, then here's a cross to bear: within a month, a good portion of Christians would be praying and memorizing the suras and verses of the Quran. "For Islam and Muslims!"

We'd finished drinking and just had a snack when the priest suddenly vomited. He managed to cover his mouth with his hands and staggered to the restroom. As if in response to a call from his soul, Monk Gregory suddenly appeared with a decanter of vodka, within which a viper lurked, ready to strike. Our table, despite the lengthy feast, retained its attractive appearance, but he still found minor imperfections, which he corrected. Then he took a large Turkish coffee pot from the table and was about to make us coffee. We stopped him, thanked him for his kind attention, and explained as best we could about the archbishop's precarious state, warning him that we were heading to the compartment to sleep.

In response, he smiled, showing white teeth, and waving his hands and moving his fingers, as if explaining with signs that everything was fine, there was no need to worry.

After brushing my teeth, I went to bed; Vladimir was gone. I fell asleep, waking up to terrifying screams and strange noises. It later emerged that passengers had caught a thief in the vestibule and were lynching him. The men were beating and torturing the unfortunate man in a crowd, while the women tried to stop the mayhem to prevent murder.

I felt really bad, in every sense of the word. I didn't have enough oxygen, the smells were irritating, I didn't want to drink or eat. I couldn't lie down or sleep. My head hurt, and my body felt like it was burning. I had never experienced such a terrible state before.

I found the strength to go to the restroom, brush my teeth, and wash my face. Then I decided to go into the restaurant and see if my fellow travelers were there. What I saw will remain etched in my memory for a long time. Sitting at the table, seemingly completely sober, were the Metropolitan and Vladimir Adamovich. Upon seeing me, they stood up and, taking turns embracing me, literally forced me to drink a hundred grams of vodka—a "penalty dose" for being late for the rest of the banquet.

We traveled like fellow sufferers, travelers on the highway. All around us, murders were being committed, violence was being perpetrated, lies were proliferating, slander and carefully dosed disinformation were spreading like a disease. We, meanwhile, drank bitter wine and analyzed: why, what for, what... Powerless to influence the processes. Only to pray.

I was once again surprised by the priest, Yakov Stepanovich in the world. Five hours ago, he was vomiting from alcohol, but now he was drinking vodka and greedily devouring a large piece of smoked fish, washing it down with a sweet black loaf. Having finished the meal, wiping his greasy hands with a napkin, the metropolitan proudly announced.

"We'll be reaching Khabarovsk in half an hour; we need to get off at the station. I need to dress appropriately for the meeting with the holy fathers; they'll greet us with due honor and gifts."

At that moment, Monk Gregory emerged from the kitchen and brought two plates of large, picture-perfect white pickled mushrooms with coarsely sliced onions to the table. Vladimir Adamovich clapped his hands and laughed. The archbishop, filling my glass with vodka from the decanter, put his arm firmly around my shoulders, and whispered softly in my ear.

- Rakhman, what do you think of Aglaya? - Do you like her? She told me she liked you.

He looked intently into my eyes, as if trying to find out my thoughts, but I couldn't find anything to answer, shrugged my shoulders and remained silent, lost in thought.

Vladimir Adamovich proposed a toast: that our trip would end well, that we would definitely go with him to visit him on Rublyovka upon arrival, and that he should introduce us to his family. Before we could raise our glasses, Grigory carried a tray of steaming hot chebureki, generously sprinkled with dill, for appetizers.

Life is filled with new impressions from current events in the world and the richness of interesting encounters with amazing people of all walks of life. And in this turmoil of personal problems, does anyone want to throw the hatchet at their neighbor?

The train, picking up speed, traveled along its designated route, its wheels clacking to the rhythm of a song playing on the television. My soul felt calm, the trembling in my body had subsided, and I could breathe easier. The news began. The announcer, in a firm voice, announced that an Israeli soldier had shot three boys point-blank in Gaza.

AYATH AL -KURSI. ALLAH - THERE IS NO DEITY BUT HIM, THE LIVING, THE SUPPORTER OF LIFE. NOR DOMB NOR SLEEP OVERCOME HIM. TO HIM BELONGS WHAT IS IN THE HEAVENS AND WHAT IS ON THE EARTH. WHO CANNOT INTERCEDE WITH HIM EXCEPT HIS PERMISSION? HE KNOWS THEIR FUTURE AND THEIR PAST. THEY UNDERSTAND FROM HIS KNOWLEDGE NONE OTHER THAN WHAT HE WILLS. HIS THRONETHER ENCOMPASSES THE HEAVENS AND THE EARTH, AND THEIR GUARDING IS NOT WEARY TO HIM. HE IS THE EXALT, THE GREAT.

With love and respect for all people in the world. Let us condemn Zionism, fascism, racism, and terrorism. Let us condemn the corrupt media, corruption, and violence of any kind. Life is given to everyone by the Almighty God in one go. It is best to live in peace.

With respect, N.M. May 5, 2007

www.ingramcontent.com/pod-product-compliance
Lightning Source LLC
LaVergne TN
LVHW011937070526
838202LV00054B/4686